SACRED JOURNEYS

Design copyright © Carlton Books Limited 2009
Text copyright © Rebecca Hind 2009

This edition published in 2009 by
Carlton Books Limited
20 Mortimer Street
London W1T 3JW

10 9 8 7 6 5 4 3 2 1

A CIP catalogue record for this book is available
from the British Library.

ISBN: 978-1-84732-272-2

Printed and bound in Dubai

Senior Executive Editor: Lisa Dyer
Senior Art Editor: Gülen Shevki-Taylor
Designer: Tyrone Taylor
Copy Editors: Nicky Gyopari and Claire Ellerton
Picture Researcher: Jenny Meredith
Production: Kate Pimm

previous page The labyrinth at Amiens
Cathedral, France (see pages 176–7).

this page The diamond throne at the
foot of the Bodhi Tree in Bodhgaya, India
(see pages 24–7).

SACRED JOURNEYS

RITUALS, ROUTES AND PILGRIMAGES TO SPIRITUAL FULFILMENT

REBECCA HIND

CARLTON
BOOKS

CONTENTS

left The Shrine of the Book, in the Israel Museum in Jerusalem,
houses the Dead Sea Scrolls found in the Qumran Caves (see pages
52–5). The building was designed to match the curves of the lids of
the clay jars the scrolls were found in.

Introduction

The landscape is full of sacred places, those bursts of luminous magnitude which, though as scattered as the stars across the heavens, are nonetheless rooted in our world. Throughout history we have sought the divine and, drawn by a sense of wonder and mystery, have found ways to forge relationships with our ineffable creator. We have gravitated towards the places where we have found the Spirit of Place – *genius loci* – and because of that essence, be it subtly sensed or known for sure, paths have been trodden to find God. The routes may be intimate or open, public or private, for the sacred is wherever we sense the divine and make contact with that which is beyond human understanding.

In the first chapter, History and Mystery, we begin by looking at the founders of faith in history and the source of inspiration that feeds pilgrimage, and which has done so for thousands of years along many of the routes taken. Some are clearly marked in the physical world while others are less tangible, and they lead us to find sacred energies within deep caves and upon soaring mountains. They trace a landscape marked by significant events, through lives lost, or knowledge found, along paths where the saints and sages worked their miracles or sensed the divine in the natural world. The Dreamtime we encounter in Australia and the ancient rock art in Botswana, take us to a places where the spiritual presence is marked upon the land itself. By contrast, the faith groups that trace their leaders and forefathers back to Jerusalem have history held in sacred texts, and their journeys are firmly rooted in still extant paths and structures. The Western Wall, the Appian Way and the scrolls found in the Qumran Caves, for example, hold compelling evidence to delight the historian and the spiritual traveller alike. However when we turn to the Eastern religions, nature is the page from which spiritual knowledge is read, and mindful wandering is the shaman's path. Natural energies are contained and epitomized by the flow of water, such as the River Ganges, that spiritual artery acknowledged by Jain, Hindu, Buddhist and Sikh.

Next we come to consider Routes and Reasons, looking at the process of setting out and what it is about the journey itself that adds to the value of arriving at a sacred destination. A journey is a course of travelling, and takes the name from the distance which could once be covered in one day; but the journey to a holy place can be of any duration, which interval may be either an all-consuming commitment or of no relevance at all. And the timing of events may be measured through the telescope, when the stars' cyclical alignments are critical and auspicious. For some, trips are made for personal growth, penitence, healing or gratitude while others set off on behalf of someone else. We see all of these aspects at Tinos in Greece, along with another – that of condensing the physical demands of a long journey into a relatively short one, by approaching the end point on hands and knees.

The third chapter, Along the Way, reminds us to be open to what we find during our journey. Every experience and each companion can teach us something, offering a chance to learn and grow from what we encounter. Furthermore, some groups deliberately use the opportunity to embed culture in their community members. For example the Huichol people of Mexico call at many sacred places along their pilgrim route and the shaman will pass wisdom found in the furl of a leaf and the whisper of breath from the forest. Different faith groups come together in Sri Pada and it interesting to note that here the pilgrimage is not deemed to be complete until the traveller has returned home, therefore the pilgrimage to this exquisite landmark is a 'round trip'. And circular movement is recognized too in Mongolia, but as having cosmic significance; to circle sunwise is to align oneself with solar and planetary paths and thus engenders harmony.

In the fourth chapter, Inner Journeys, Sacred Realms, we reflect upon the inner dimension so essential to spiritual progression – for the divine is recognized by that part inside of us which longs to know the realms beyond our grasp. These are the places to which we reach when we pray and when we share rituals and sacraments. And reaching inside can be aided by the varied chants and mantras employed by monks down the ages, which resonate with sacred vibration, such as that which is encapsulated in the syllable om, the sound of the universe uttered at Buddhist and Hindu sites. Elsewhere, the sacred choral music of the great cathedrals and abbeys, at Amiens, Fátima and Iona, generates mystical power to fill the heart and lift the spirit.

Reaching the end of the sacred journey is not the end of the pilgrim's progress however. Arrival brings with it the need to rest perhaps, and then to fulfil the purpose of the journey, whatever that may be, and to celebrate. Celebration is often formalized into ritual and may re-enact an event from history, such as the processions of Holy Week in Seville, as seen in the final chapter Arrivals and Rituals. And then there is the choice between turning around and moving off again, or staying at the destination. Either way, a new start is being made.

right The jagged teeth of the entrance to the Pak Ou Caves in Laos offer a dramatic approach to the darkness and surprises within, where there are shrines filled with Buddhist figures both large and small. The caves are only accessible by boat from Luang Prabang.

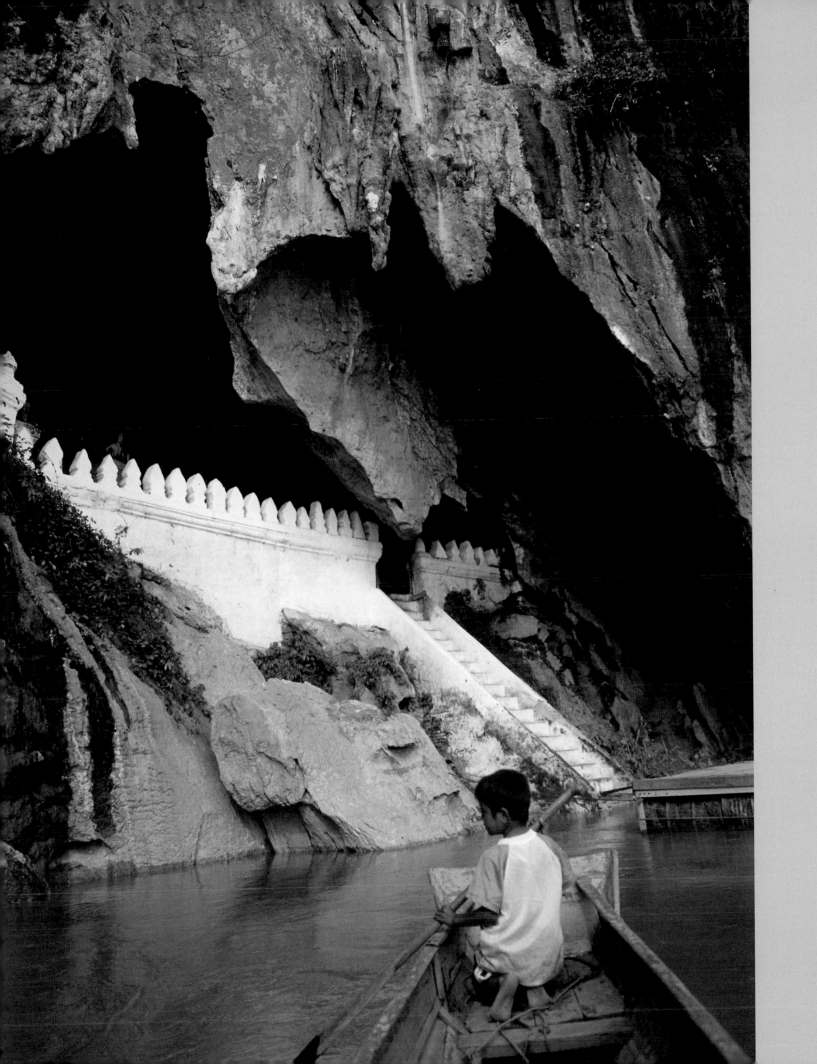

The sacred journeys that span our world have evolved over thousands of years. They have been loved and used, carved and cared for, marked and smoothed. In some cases they have been lost and found. And in return they have guided, comforted, challenged and inspired us. They have found their way into literature and art just as those human expressions have beckoned travellers away from home and onto the road, into the air or across the seas. Through all of those elements, pilgrimages will ever be made. For although many of journeys are rooted in the ancient past, they still bear fruit for today's pilgrims, are still relevant and vibrant. Between these pages is something of the essence of sacred journeys. May yours be fulfilling and your arrivals joyful.

above The Potala Palace at Lhasa in Tibet, also known as the Sunlit City, rises 117 metres (384 feet) from the valley floor. Pilgrims move clockwise through the building and must never stand on a threshold. Built to be the official residence of the Dalai Lama, now exiled in India, the palace has now been converted to a museum.

left The paths to Santiago de Compostela in Spain are varied and pass through many types of landscape. Here we see a gentle incline and leafy shade, but travellers must be prepared for all forms of terrain and weather.

HISTORY AND MYSTERY

The history of sacred journeys is veiled by time, though each account offers clues to its roots. As scholars, historians and archaeologists filter through what has come to light, traces emerge to give us glimpses of our early quests for spiritual transformation through travel. The development of sacred paths and practices is described using many different means, according to the various faiths' traditions.

left The late Pope John Paul II is seen here in Saint Peter's Basilica, in Rome. The basilica is among the most venerated of Christian sites outside the Holy Land. Ranks of bishops, clergy, choir and laity unite in worship within these hallowed walls. Countless sacred journeys have begun and ended here, many aided by the glorious art and architecture, which nourishes faith and lifts the soul.

In Australia the Aboriginals' sacred journeys trace the threads of Dreamtime, the spiritual 'time before time' when the Ancestral Spirits created all things; wherever these shape-shifting spirits travelled, so they marked the land, creating rivers and mountains, flora and fauna in what is celebrated as Songlines. These concepts of Dreaming and Songlines may be abstract to outsiders, but they are culturally embedded, passed by painted narrative, ritual and oral tradition. In some instances, the young are taught through rock art or body painting, made with pigment that has been gathered at the end of a sacred journey.

By contrast, we find the origins of Jewish pilgrimage to the Temple in Jerusalem, held and told in the pages of the Old Testament, which, from the days of King David, called all men over the age of 13 to make pilgrimage to honour religious custom there. This practice is still thriving some 3,000 years on, despite the difficulties that have arisen over time. For Christians, the first famous sacred journeys involved Christ's birth and early years. His family's trip to Bethlehem, the visiting Magi and the escape into Egypt are just a few, but more poignant is His later walk from Jerusalem to Golgotha, burdened by the cross and

the prospect of its purpose. This journey is widely re-enacted in various forms across the globe. And Jerusalem is the place that marks the start of Mohammed's night journey to Mecca, the greatest Muslim pilgrim site, to which the faithful turn five times each day for prayer, and where hajjis gather in their millions.

Each of the faiths connected to Jerusalem is blessed by a dependable written heritage, sacred texts which have formed the basis of spiritual practice and pinpointed hallowed ground. The Holy Land is also sacred to the Bahá'í, whose prophet Baha'ullah came here from nineteenth century Persia and wrote of the divine revelations he experienced. He identified places to pray and his words are safely stored for all to study. In China, Taoists look to the words of the *Tao Te Ching*, or *The Way*, for wisdom. Written around the sixth century BC, it has been a pivotal influence on Chinese thinking, within Buddhism as well as Taoism. Lao tzu was the founder of Taoism and possible author of *The Way*.

Sites connected with the Buddha's life and teaching are all auspicious places to pray and we know that he too

travelled widely, leaving venerated footprints in his wake. He preached in Varanasi, drawn to the site's already established propitiousness, and declared it as a place of pilgrimage for his followers; in doing so he broadened its spiritual status further still and multiplied the pilgrim numbers. Many paths meet up in Varanasi, which had been a place of ritual worship for Hindus long before the Buddha arrived. Sikhs and Jains gather here too, joining in with festivals such as Deepavali (also known as Diwali).

 All of these faiths have sacred texts and art forms through which they can read the map of holy travel and decipher something of the wonders of faith and sacred practice. For followers of Shinto, there are fewer tangible pointers, though the ancient *Kojiki* text tells of creation myths. Mindful wandering in nature has always led followers to find the divine within the quiet breath of the elements, and sacred chanting, dance and ritual honour the Way of the Kami, the innumerable sacred life energies. These Shinto traditions evolved through mythology, and the interpretive skills of the shaman, who communicates via divination with the spirit. Native Americans also retreat into nature when they seek a vision quest, and await messages sent by the Great Spirit; here too the shaman is an intermediary.

Within each faith group, charismatic figures have inspired others to follow them, both in conduct and by beating a path to find encouragement by association. Thus, hermitages, chapels, glades and caves frequented by the saints and sages act as spiritual magnets, with distance and duration proving to be no deterrent. What goes on in the mind and soul is intangible, ineffable and, by definition, the mystery of faith. Seekers of spiritual truth follow the guidance of their mentors, the word of spiritual texts, and transforming ritual, according to their faith. Wherever on earth this guidance may lead, it aims to cure the soul and bring harmony to the world, and to all that dwell here. The ultimate goal is that mysterious state called paradise, nirvana, heaven or the hereafter.

left to right Mount Tai, Shandong Province, China; the Hajj, Mecca, Saudi Arabia; the Western Wall, Jerusalem, Israel; Tsodilo, the Kalahari Desert, Botswana.

Walkabout at Narran Lake
New South Wales, Australia

'Walkabout' is the Australian Aboriginals' name for sacred travel. It is also, arguably, the oldest form of sacred journey and a term that belies the activity's complexity. For Walkabout follows the threads of Songlines that invisibly cross the landscape, binding the human, physical and sacred worlds, linking the past to the present and to the future. This is a web too complex and esoteric for outsiders to ever fully understand; indeed, many of the traditions are held tightly within the Aboriginal culture. To follow the Songlines re-establishes the stories and traditions that have underpinned the culture here since the Dreamtime – that realm of creation when people were made and the landscape was first steeped in the sacred energy that still exists today.

It was in Dreamtime that the great spirit father, Baiame, went hunting and left his two wives gathering food. As they awaited his return, the women decided to refresh themselves in the clear waters of Coorigal Springs. At once, they were seized by two Kurreahs, the giant crocodiles that stalked the waters at that time. As the Kurreahs made off, they took the women and the waters with them. On his return, Baiame found the women's skirts by the dried-up spring and guessed what had befallen his wives. So he set off in pursuit of the unhappy party, running from one dried-up water hole to the next. Luckily, he was able to outwit the creatures and get ahead by cutting across the bends, meeting the beasts head on with his spear. In the fury of the ensuing battle the Kurreahs' angry thrashing scooped a hollow in the mud, which filled with the waters they had brought and thus was formed the Narran Lake. Baiame cut the creatures open and retrieved his wives, who recovered, but never again swam in those waters.

Ten thousand years ago, all living things were instructed by Baiame to wait for him at the lake. There he inscribed a sacred circle, or bora, which represented his physical form, from which all life springs, and thus the circle was established as a symbol of initiation and creation.

Since that time boras, where sacred energy is found to collect, have been made and used as ritual sites all across Australia. The circle may be marked by stone, earth mounds or compacted by the tread of feet according to local tradition, but it is to these secret places that boys travel for the sacred rites of passage through which they symbolically cross into manhood, away from the eyes of their womenfolk. Today the Narran Lake Nature Reserve is protected and valued for its status as a wetland of international importance. The area encompasses a network of river channels, lakes and flood plain, all of which allow the flow of life-giving energy to journey still across this sacred landscape.

left Narran Lakes Nature Reserve has traditional and contemporary spiritual value for the Aboriginal people of the area. It is also home to many species of internationally valued waterfowl due to the wealth of its waters, which run across a wide flood plain. This watery flux is a site of invisible sacred energies, the Songlines, which weave between the earthly and spirit worlds.

above Kurreahs, such as this one painted on bark, were giant crocodiles of the Dreamtime. They prowled the wetlands around this landscape and once made off with the wives of the spirit father, Baiame, taking the waters with them. When he caught up with them, the angry thrashing of their tales scooped the ground and formed the Narran Lake.

right Aboriginal people use earth pigments to express and communicate with spirits of the natural world, such as these Dreamtime figures and Barramundi fish. The process of collecting and preparing the pigments is itself an ancient sacred ritual.

The Western Wall

Jerusalem, Israel

Christians revere Jerusalem because of Jesus' ministry, crucifixion and resurrection here; for Muslims it is Al-Quds, the Holy, and the starting point of Mohammed's night journey to Mecca and his subsequent ascent through the seven heavens. It is one of the oldest cities in the world and, for Jews, the most sacred. King David founded it in the hope of uniting the surrounding tribes and making it a spiritual focus for the Jewish people. Solomon, King David's son, built the first temple here in the tenth century BC. From the time of the Babylonian invasion in 587 BC there have been repeated conquests, disputes and war. The Jewish revolt against the Romans began in AD 66 and the second temple was razed during AD 70, with only the Western Wall left standing.

The Jewish tradition of pilgrimage to Jerusalem is called *aliyah*, or ascent. According to the Torah, or Jewish teaching, men over the age of 13 should make a pilgrimage to Jerusalem three times a year to mark agricultural cycles and, symbolically, historical events. As the books of Exodus and Deuteronomy state, during the month in which the Jews left Egypt they should celebrate the Festival of Unleavened Bread, then the Festival of Harvest, followed by the Festival of Shelters when the fruits are gathered. And they should do so by coming to God, because 'Every year at these three festivals all your men must come to worship me, the Lord your God' (Exodus 23:17). Thus pilgrimage to the temple began. However, since the temple's destruction, the remaining Western Wall is

now deemed to hold something of its sanctity and is thus the Jews' most poignant site, or spiritual home. Tradition tells that construction of the temple was shared among the various sectors of the community, the poor having responsibility for this part. Unable to pay for workmen, they built it with their own hands, an act which gave the wall the protection of angels when the rest of the temple was destroyed.

While pilgrimage was once a time for sacrificial offering, in the absence of a temple this can no longer happen and so lament replaced that ritual and the soubriquet 'Wailing Wall' was adopted. Pilgrims may slip written invocations into the wall itself where intercession, supplication and devotion can be absorbed into the prayers of those who came before. The prayer shawl, or tallit, is worn as an enveloping reminder that one is constantly under God's wing, and men wear tefillin, small leather boxes containing inscriptions from the Torah, one on the head and one on the arm, as reminders of their Covenant with God. Although Jerusalem is now large, the Old City covers less than one kilometre square (²⁄₅ square mile) and packed with key religious pilgrimage sites. These, and their collective histories, symbolism and witness make Jerusalem a spiritual powerhouse and yet, sadly, one of the most contentious places on earth. However, it should be noted that despite the undoubted darkness that Jerusalem has witnessed, the light of sacred devotion has never been extinguished.

far left The area around the Western Wall, which is also known as the Kotel, functions as a great, open-air synagogue. As such it is a place for prayer, teaching and discourse. Men of the different traditions of Judaism meet here, along with men from all age groups. The lower, larger stones in the wall are ancient; they date from 20 BC, the time of King Herod.

centre Between the lower stones, pilgrims slip written prayers. In this way their prayers come into direct contact with the sacred, as have the prayers of all who worshipped here before. It is said that during the 11 years it took to build the walls, rain fell only at night, so as not to delay the builders' work.

left Jewish women are not allowed to pray with men at the Western Wall, but form their own prayer groups instead. This tradition is currently being challenged by women's groups who declare that the wall is a symbol of Jewish survival and that therefore there should be equal access to it. This debate is the subject of a 2008 documentary made by Yael Katzir, *Praying in Her Own Voice*.

overleaf The prayer shawl, or tallit, is worn as a symbol of the wearer being constantly under God's protection. The garment is also a reminder of His commandments and, being made to traditional designs, contains symbolic language. It is worn during morning prayer on the Sabbath and holidays.

Mount Tai
Shandong Province, China

Mount Tai, or Taishan, was first inhabited by humans in the Neolithic period and traces of man's activity here date back to Palaeolithic times. Standing at 1,545 metres (5,069 feet), Taishan is the highest peak in the province and sometimes called Chief of the Five Sacred Mountains of Taoism, although it is not only its height that makes it significant. According to the Spring and Autumn periods of China's history, east signifies birth and springtime, thus, standing at the eastern side of the North China Plain, Taishan is seen as the most auspicious mountain and people have come here to worship for 3,000 years. Covering 550 square kilometres (212 square miles), Mount Tai is endowed with a profound and prodigious natural beauty. And during those three millennia it has evinced the creative presence and moved poets, painters and architects to some of China's finest artistic expression.

Along with more than 100 buildings of various ages and functions, and 1,800 stones bearing inscriptions of masterly poetic and philosophical expression, there are all manner of devotional works. For example, the rocks themselves bear carved inscriptions, such as the Buddhist *Diamond*

left Pilgrims toil up the Stairway to Heaven leading to the Gateway to Heaven at the top of Mount Tai. The mountain reaches 1,545 metres (5,069 feet), the highest in the province, thus closest to paradise.

below Near the top of the mountain rests Azure Clouds Temple. There are 7,000 steps leading to the top. Each section offers a different view, encouraging climbers on their way. Here we look down on the temple as the morning sun casts its rays over the architecture of the building.

Sutra cut over 1,400 years ago, while the Tiankuang Hall holds a huge mural entitled *The God of Mount Tai Making a Journey*, painted in 1009. Religious worship here began with ceremonies honouring the earth at the foot of the mountain and heaven and the sun on its peak. Passing between those two stations became, over time, a ritual journey in its own right, taken by emperors and pilgrims from far and wide. In fact the first emperor, Qin Shi Huang, thought the mountain summit so significant that it was from here in 219 BC that he ceremonially announced the unity of the empire. A tradition arose following the Song dynasty (960–1279) of taking stones from the mountain to act as talismans, in the belief that the mountain's physical matter must carry its sacred powers. By setting these stones in auspicious places, perhaps formed into tablets and inscribed, a community could enjoy peace and protection from danger. In this way, the mountain's potency reaches beyond its footprint to those who cannot travel.

For those who can manage it, being at the top for dawn offers a view of the world awakening as the sun breathes life into the landscape, tinting heaven and earth with vibrant colour and leading the eye to focus on the physical world and the spirit on what is beyond. Lower down, pilgrims are surrounded by a unique landscape lush with flora, fauna and geology, which have won this landscape its geopark status. The imperial route is still used, beginning at the Yaocan Pavilion and passing a number of significant temples, gateways and natural features on the way; these are the tangible features of the mountain. The life span of the ancient trees, the sounds of the streams, the cloud formations, swirling mists, shifting colours and scents are the subtle elements that combine to stimulate the senses into recognizing the numinous and making this an obvious focus for Taoist and Buddhist worship.

left above At the Heavenly Gate, couples lock their love for all eternity by fastening a padlock, often inscribed with their names, and throwing away the key. This traditional affirmation of making a shared promise and binding it to hallowed ground is seen at many sacred points in China, especially on mountains, and the tradition is finding its way around the world.

left below Early visitors reach the Heavenly Gate at the top of the mountain at sunrise. A gate heralds a point of arrival and passing through it symbolizes the entering of a new realm, in this case the kingdom of heaven. Facing east and the morning sun, the mountain symbolizes birth and springtime. Its position, aspect and height all contribute to the mountain's auspiciousness.

right Looking back along the stairway, it is possible to see people of all ages come and go at their own pace. The great mountain asserts its authority and the wisdom of years. And here, clinging to the mountainside, is a path balanced on the edge of creation, the cusp of the known world falling away beside the path to heaven.

The Bodhi Tree
Bodhgaya, India

This spot marks the place at which the Lord Buddha reached the state of enlightenment, and although we cannot be sure of the Buddha's exact dates, his followers and historians agree that he lived during the sixth or fifth century BC, making this a truly ancient pilgrim site. Shortly after his birth it was predicted that prince Siddhartha would become either a powerful king or a great spiritual leader. Hoping for the former, his royal parents gave the boy a sheltered life of privilege. However, he became spiritually inquisitive and on witnessing the hardship of many outside the palace he vowed to seek a route to deliverance from worldly suffering. Inspired by the serenity of a wandering monk, Siddhartha decided to adopt the itinerant lifestyle for himself, took the name Gautama and left the palace. After six years of asceticism, Gautama arrived at Bodhgaya and found himself drawn to sit within the shade of a pipal tree, vowing not to leave until he had found enlightenment. There, facing east, he meditated for 49 days, finally reaching the spiritual enlightenment known to Buddhists as nirvana. Having arrived at this epiphany the monk became known as the Buddha or the Awakened One, and people came from far and wide in the hope of gaining something of the spiritual power the site clearly held. As word of this event spread the tree became famous and was named the Sacred Fig, Bodhi or Bo Tree. Pilgrims took its seeds away with them and the new trees and their offspring mark out those sacred journeys to this day. Because of the significance of what the tree helped to engender, many regard the ground in which it was rooted as the world's centre, the source of all enlightenment, the state to which all Buddhists aspire.

Unsurprisingly then, the temple draws hoards of people who come for a multitude of reasons. And though they come on ordinary days to pray for their family, community or the world, they come too for organized events such as the annual Buddha Jayanti Festival. This honours the Buddha's birth, enlightenment and nirvana in a colourful event of celebratory processions, dancing, the symbolic lighting of candles, the chanting of prayers and meditation. Two hundred and fifty years after the Buddha's enlightenment, King Ashoka, a devotee who actively spread Buddhism, journeyed here and established the

right This diamond throne marks the seat of enlightenment where, beneath a sacred tree, Gautama sat meditating. Mara, the Lord of Illusion, tried to distract him, but Gautama touched the earth, asking it to attest to his many lives of virtue. The earth shook and Mara unleashed demons which, in the ensuing battle, turned into flowers. Mara fled and Gautama gained enlightenment.

first temple, the Mahabodhi Temple. The building we see today dates from the fifth and sixth centuries and exhibits the technical and artistic genius of architects and craftworkers in the late Gupta period. These artworks not only narrate the Buddhist stories but also convey their essence in delightfully expressive three-dimensional

form. It is said that one of Ashoka's children took a cutting from the original tree to Sri Lanka where it grew into the Sri Maha Bodi. This, in turn, was propagated and a seedling returned to the Mahabodhi Temple. Today its branches spread like embracing arms, beneath which today's pilgrims pray and seek their own enlightenment.

below A pilgrim sits absorbed in quiet meditation by the Bodhi Tree. She wears white, the colour of learning, which transforms ignorance into wisdom. The lineage of this Bodhi Tree can be traced back to the original tree beneath which Gautama gained enlightenment. It is thus considered to be representative of the Buddha himself, through the physical connection.

right The elaborate Mahabodhi Temple is 52 metres (170 feet) high on a square base of 15 metres (49 feet). It is a monument to the Buddha's enlightenment. The narrow, pyramidal form is called a *shikhara*. It houses a huge sculpture of the Buddha touching the ground in meditation, which is thought to be 1,700 years old. It faces east, the direction of enlightenment.

above Monks attend the Kagyu Monlam, an annual prayer ceremony
seeking worldwide peace and harmony. The symbolism of colour plays
an important role in Buddhist visual language. The saffron robes of these
Buddhist monks represent rootedness to the earth and renunciation. Yellow
is a nourishing colour associated with turning pride into wisdom.

above The Kagyu Monlam ceremony is attended by monks, lamas, nuns and laity. The sacred red in which these monks are dressed represents blood, the life force and therefore preservation. It aids discernment and is associated with fire. Fixing on a colour during meditation is believed to help concentration and therefore spiritual growth.

The Appian Way
Rome, Italy

Rome has stood on hallowed ground for at least 2,500 years. We know this because the city's sacred spaces and buildings sit layer upon layer, compressing and preserving the spectrum of worship and dedication that underpins twenty-first century devotional practice. Roman gods were honoured here from around 575 BC and today's Jewish community can trace its establishment to 161 BC with the advent of envoys from Judea. Christianity arrived during the first century AD with Christ's apostles Peter and Paul, who were both martyred here. Thus Rome became and continues to be an important pilgrim destination for Christians of all denominations.

left The fusion of art and architecture in Saint Peter's Basilica is second to none. Over its long history it has accumulated a wealth of symbolism, narrative and sacred symbols which grace every surface from floor to dome. Here at the crossing, we see the dome rising to 138 metres (453 feet), supported by huge decorated pillars which are over 18 metres (59 feet) thick.

below Here in Saint Peter's Square we see thousands of people attending Holy Mass, celebrated by the Pope. Yet even this great crowd is dwarfed by the towering basilica, crowned by its great dome. A site of ancient significance, generations of Christians have come here to honour Saint Peter, whose tomb is said to lie beneath the high altar within.

Tradition holds that Peter arrived in Rome via the Appian Way – the road stretching across from Brindisi, the port on the Adriatic coast that greeted arrivals from the Hellenic world. It is said that when fleeing Roman persecution by that same route, Peter had a vision of meeting Christ, which gave him the courage to turn around and face his martyrdom. This event is commemorated by the Chiesa del Domine Quo Vadis. After his death by crucifixion, Peter's remains lay for a time with those of Paul in the catacombs, also on the Appian Way. So although this road was built by the Romans about 300 years before Christ's followers arrived, it has become a route dotted with tombs, catacombs and chapels leading Christians to this eternal city.

Another Roman site now revered by Christians is Saint Peter's Basilica, which stands on what was once the Circus of Nero, an arena set aside for the slaughter of Christians, including Saint Peter himself. Christianity was formally adopted during the fourth century by Constantine the Great, the first Roman emperor to embrace Christianity. It was he who marked this site with the first basilica during AD 324 and huge numbers of people now come here to what is among the most venerated of Christian sites outside the Holy Land. Indeed, it was Constantine who promoted religious tolerance throughout the Roman Empire, paving the way for those who come to seek, deepen or celebrate their faith. Today's basilica, begun in 1546, has a capacity

of 60,000 and an astonishing number of features including chapels, grottoes and monuments. Furthermore, it houses a wealth of work made by some of Italy's finest artists and craftworkers. For example, in the Pieta Chapel, Michelangelo's sculpture of the dead Christ being lamented by his mother provides an intensely moving devotional image; the Blessed Sacrament Chapel was decorated by Bernini and, for many, gazing at his angels on the altar leads them to an understanding of spiritual truths expressed as transcendent beauty. Religious art imparts a range of ideas and stories that can lead us deeper into the mystery of the Christian journey by virtue of a language capable of articulating that which lies beyond words. Linking all of the art, the gilding, the polished marble and the saints and martyrs honoured here are the sacred threads which draw so many to journey to Rome from across the globe.

far left Within the splendid interior of the Basilica of Santa Croce di Gerusalemme are artworks by some of Italy's finest masters, including frescoes of the *Legends of the True Cross*, attributed to Melozzo. There is also an icon reputedly made for Pope Gregory I after he was visited by a vision of Christ, along with an exact replica of the Turin Shroud.

left The Basilica of Santa Croce di Gerusalemme is one of Rome's seven pilgrim churches. Consecrated around AD 325, its floor was strewn with soil from Calvary, or Golgotha; thus it was sufficiently sacred to house the Passion Relics, also from the Holy Land.

below Here Pope Benedict XVI presides at Corpus Domini, a celebration in which the consecrated bread of the Eucharist is carried through the streets in procession. Eucharistic bread and wine are received during Holy Communion and represent Christ's life flowing into the communicant's.

Varanasi
Uttar Pradesh, India

Known also as Benaras or Kashi, this city on the banks of the Ganges is a place buzzing with ancient mythology and culture, drawing visitors by virtue of its sacred cosmic power; to journey here is to tread a sacred path to liberation. According to the Hindu text *Vamana Purana*, two tributaries of the river Ganges, Varuna and Assi, flowed from the beginning of time and the land between them is Kashi, meaning shrine. In mythology this is the ground upon which the gods Shiva and Parvati stood at that moment of creation, making this place forever sacred and one of the most auspicious sites for Hindus since antiquity.

In Hindu belief, bathing in the river Ganges is an act of spiritual cleansing; dying in Varanasi releases the soul from the cycle of life, death and rebirth. Ghats, the steps and terraces lining parts of the river, allow access to the water, and by offering that space are themselves sacred places; people use them to offer prayers to the morning sun, to release the ashes of their dead and to cleanse themselves in the waters of the mother goddess. Many of the ghats have distinct qualities. For instance, the Hindu poet Tulsidas (*c.* 1543–1623) lived here and lends his name to the Tulsi Ghat. His version of the ancient literary epic, the *Ramayana*, which he called the Lake of the Deeds of Rama, has inspired a multitude of interpretations of that story. It is thought that the *Ramayana*, a tale of the seventh incarnation of Vishnu, was first performed in Varanasi. Performances fuse many elements of the city's culture. Sacred dance, for example, is given for the gods' enjoyment and, for the dancers, is a route to salvation. Numerous festivals here celebrate and narrate mythology through theatre, music, poetry, prose and the visual arts. Artisans spin, dye and weave the most luscious silks in vivid colours that speak of the joys of creation; the material world pulses with colour as sun and fire play across its surfaces. This is expressed most particularly in the Dev Deepavali – the Light Festival of the Gods. At this time, over one million earthenware lamps are lit next to the river to welcome the deities as they descend to earth, greeted by prayer and hymn singing as light triumphs over darkness. Coinciding with the full moon this joyful, sparkling festival is also concurrent with the Sikh celebrations for Guru Nanak Jayanti (the Guru's birthday) and the Jain Festival of Light, which marks the nirvana of Lord Mahavira in 527 BC. Jains are included among the one million visitors who come here each year, along with Buddhist pilgrims who also recognize and celebrate the sanctity of the waters, temples and rituals. In fact the Buddha himself nominated Varanasi as a pilgrim destination and it was in the deer park here that he first preached of Buddhist truths and practice. The holy city's rich sacred origins breathe the energy of creation into the varied spectrum of Varanasi people and pilgrims; they return it through inspired worship.

above Standing praying in the waters of the holy Ganges, one woman takes a moment for personal silence, quietly withdrawing from the bustle around her. Stepping into the waters here is an act of devotion and ritual cleansing at a place honoured over countless centuries. Many will hope to receive *darshan* here – eye contact with a holy one which conveys a special blessing.

right Greeting the morning sun is one of the delightful sacred ceremonies to which pilgrims flock. There is no restriction on who may come – Sikhs, Jains and Buddhists join the Hindu faithful as the waters, which embody the mother goddess Ganga, flow with blessings. Many people fill vessels with holy water to take away for those unable to get here themselves.

right Agni is the Hindu god of fire. Sacrifices made to him lead straight to the deities as he is both the receiver and messenger of all that is surrendered heavenwards. Eternal, he is also forever youthful, as his flames can be rekindled to infinity. Fire ceremonies are observed at all major festivals and rites of passage.

far right An ancient festival of light, Divali takes its name from the Sanskrit word *deepavali*, or 'row of lamps'. It is marked by the lighting of *deeyas*, clay lamps burning oil or ghee. The festival has its roots in the ancient tale of the *Ramayana* and symbolizes the triumph of good over bad. The appeal of flickering lamps is a timeless mystery.

The Hajj
Mecca, Saudi Arabia

Pilgrims have come to the holy city of Mecca since the days of the prophet Abraham, and today's Hajj (pilgrimage) refers to events during his life with Hagar, his wife, and Ishmael, their son. These events would also be recognized by Jews and Christians as they are recorded in the Old Testament of the Bible, but only Muslims may make sacred journeys here now. Each year increasing numbers of pilgrims make the Hajj, around three million in recent years, travelling to the birthplace of the Prophet Mohammed from across the globe. Attending at least once in a lifetime is considered a duty, one of the Five Pillars of Islam, for all who can afford it.

Pilgrims arrive during the last month of the year, Dhu al-Hijja, and the traveller's rituals begin outside Mecca by changing from everyday clothes into special white garments. By dressing in this way the pilgrim, or hajji, enters a state of ihram, which represents spiritual cleanliness, the shedding of worldly matters, and equality before God. The hajji may now enter the city. At the core of the great al-Harām mosque is the focus of this pilgrimage, the Kaaba. This ancient, pre-Islamic shrine is thought by Muslims to have first been built by Abraham and his son Ishmael. Over time, it has been rebuilt by various ruling tribes as a place of worship and a house for sacred

left Throngs of pilgrims circumnavigate the Kaaba seven times during the Hajj. The Kaaba stands at the heart of the Al-Masjid al-Harām, the Holy Mosque, which is the world's largest. The Haram was first built during the seventh century. It has evolved into its current form gradually through frequent expansion and modification, according to increased pilgrim numbers.

below Qibla is the direction for prayer. Worshippers face in this direction, pointing towards the Kaaba, whenever they want to pray. The Kaaba, seen here at the centre of the picture, is also the centre of the world in Islamic tradition, and considered the most holy object. Built into the side of the Kaaba is the mysterious Black Stone.

objects, including the Black Stone. This mysterious stone of unknown age and origin was kissed by Mohammed himself and is thought to have been turned black by absorbing the sins of the countless people who have kissed it over the centuries, leaving them cleansed of impurity. While there is no obligation to honour the stone in this way, many believe that it represents the primordial link between God and his people and is the cornerstone of this holy place.

The Hajj is made up of a number of rituals, which not only complement one another but also represent the essence of Islamic faith and imprint its stories on those who take part. Once the Kaaba has been circled seven times, the observance continues with sermons and symbolic activity. This includes running to re-enact Hagar's biblical journey between the hills of Safa and Marwa in her search to find water for her son; water was revealed to her at the Zamzam Well, and now, drinking from the well is said to cure hunger and illness as well as thirst. Stones are thrown at walls representing Satan and an animal is slaughtered in thanks to God for sending a sheep for Abraham to sacrifice in place of his own son. Hajjis stand in prayer on the plain of Arafat, whence Mohammed gave his farewell sermon during the last year of his life. Finally, the Kaaba is circled three more times and the faithful go on their way, having fulfilled what may have been the journey of a lifetime and a tangible link with the history of the prophets.

left On the second day of the Hajj, pilgrims move to the Mount of Mercy from whence the Prophet delivered his last sermon and asked God to forgive all who would stand there. Thus 'the standing' is a significant part of the Hajj ritual, which leaves pilgrims joyfully free from sin.

right Ihram is the white garment representing spiritual purity and equality before God. The pilgrims to the front of the picture study and pray while others 'stand before Allah' in a ritual known as *waqfa*. At sunset, each pilgrim will gather seven pebbles for the symbolic stoning of Satan on the third day.

left Hajjis in ihram pray at sunset. This scene at Mina shows evening lights over the pilgrims' encampment outside Mecca, and helps us to understand something of the scale of the pilgrimage, and of the atmosphere here. While some prostrate themselves with foreheads to the ground, others stand and remember Mohammed's last sermon within this sacred landscape.

right Pilgrims collect the pure, clear Zamzam water to drink and to take home for family and friends. Tradition holds that Jibril (the angel Gabriel) generated the spring for Hagar, in her plight. The well was excavated by hand and water was originally hoisted by bucket and rope, but nowadays pilgrims find it pumped to fountains within the mosque.

below Towards the end of the Hajj, the running ceremony, or *sa'y*, recalls Hagar's search for water for her infant child Ishmael. She frantically ran back and forth seven times between two hills until at last she found the miraculous Zamzam water, which now pools in a marble chamber beneath the Kaaba.

Bahá'í World Centre
Haifa, Israel

The newness of this destination reflects the age of the Bahá'í faith for which it is so significant. However, standing as it does on Mount Carmel, it links directly with an ancient sacred heritage common to the Abrahamic religions, and possibly even earlier prehistoric civilizations. Baha'ullah, father of the Bahá'í faith, named this site as the final resting place of the Bab, his forerunner, and as the centre for administration of a new global community. Pilgrims come here to honour the Shrine of the Bab, to study texts and archives and to bask in the beauty and symbolism of the architecture and extensive gardens, which were opened to the public in 2001.

It was in Shiraz during 1844 that a young man named Siyyid Ali Mohammed took the title Bab. Bab is the Arabic word for 'gateway', which implies arrival, in this case a revelation of God to mankind, bringing with it the long-awaited peace anticipated by religions everywhere; the Bab had been sent to prepare the way for a new messenger who would be the prophet for the coming age. However, this announcement was seen as a threat to the Muslim faith in Persia and persecution followed, with the Bab facing public execution in Tabriz in 1850. Twenty thousand of his followers in the Babi movement were also killed.

One who was captured but not slain, however, was Husayn Ali. He escaped death because of his family's status and increasing interest from the outside world. He was thrown into the notorious Black Pit for four months during 1852. This vile, stinking subterranean prison must have been a sharp and cruel contrast to his background of wealth and privilege. However, it was while in here that he experienced the religious revelations that formed the sacred texts of the Bahá'í faith. Here was the messenger anticipated by the Bab, the one who became known as Baha'ullah, meaning the 'glory of God'. On release from gaol he was exiled for 40 years, during which time he journeyed to Baghdad, Kurdistan, Constantinople (Istanbul), Adrianople (Edirne) and finally to Acre in Israel, which was then an unwholesome penal city. During this time, Baha'ullah was writing, recording his revelations and teaching, laying the code of conduct for his followers while his reputation grew and reached outwards. Furthermore, he wrote to world leaders appealing to them to settle differences and work for universal peace. Towards the end of his life certain freedoms were allowed, but in 1892 he passed away and was buried in gardens adjoining his last dwelling place in Bahji, just outside Acre. At Haifa we see a series of curved and gardened terraces which flow to the golden-domed Shrine of the Bab, then on to the top of Mount Carmel. The planting has a formality that softens to informality, then wild garden, as it ripples outwards from the shrine. The proximity of focus around the monument directs the mind towards a reverential approach and the change of style reflects the diversity of God's people and creation.

above Bahá'ís who make pilgrimages to the Holy Land must spend time in prayer and meditation at the Shrine of the Bab. The opportunity to do so is both a sacred duty and a privilege. This distinctive landmark attracts millions of visitors annually. Many are pilgrims, some are tourists; all must be touched by the eloquent yearning for peace and harmony, which radiate from the site.

left The extensive gardens of the Bahá'í World Centre were opened during 2001, and these terraces and steps rise in verdant splendour towards the Shrine of the Bab on sacred Mount Carmel. The pacific grounds epitomize the Bahá'í faith's ideals of global peace and harmony, and act as an essential oasis of calm within this deeply troubled land.

above right Within the shrine is a place for prayer and meditation. The Bahá'í faith has no formal liturgy or ceremony, but the Tablet of Visitation is a prayer stone found inside for all to use. No pilgrim here will be directionless: the faith puts a strong emphasis on study and has a number of sacred texts which deal with matters mystical, social and ethical.

Tsodilo

Kalahari Desert, Botswana

If the deities give their permission, then archaeologists may have access, via the Bushmen, to the python cave in the Tsodilo hills. And it is wise to seek their blessing. When Sir Laurens van der Post visited the area to research his book, *The Lost World of the Kalahari*, his cameras and tape recorders failed and his party was plagued by bees for three consecutive days until he planted, beneath some ave paintings, a written apology for arriving without due respect for etiquette.

Called the Mountains of the Gods, or the Rock that Whispers, Tsodilo, in the Kalahari Desert, is the canvas on which over 4,500 cave paintings have been made, in an area measuring only 10 square

below More than 4,500 paintings grace the surfaces of these cliffs and caves in the Kalahari Desert, earning this collection of rock art the name 'the Louvre of the Desert'. Local communities know the region to be the home of their ancestral spirits and the hills have a history of human activity, which is up to 100,000 years old.

right Art has always made its presence felt at sites of spiritual significance, be it painting, sculpture, music or dance. And while much of it is ephemeral, we are fortunate to have a global heritage of sacred art that has endured. While these images may inspire wonder and joy, they can also offer us a window into the sacred realms of those who first found faith.

kilometres (4 square miles). The rock paintings give the world an account of man's ritual activity over a period of 100,000 years. The people who live in this region know it to be the dwelling place of their ancestors, and as such a spiritual site of worship and sanctity. The hills take their name from the Hambukushu term for 'sheer'; collectively, the four forms represent the site of creation. In order of descending size and significance they have long been nominated male, female and child, with the fourth hill representing the male's first wife whom he discarded. Near the top of the Male Hill is the place of invocation for the first spirit at the time of creation, his knees having permanently indented the rock as he prayed. The Female Hill is both the resting place of the dead and the power base of the ruling gods. Hoof prints high upon this hill show that the god Nyambe brought the Hambukushu people to earth here.

One cave in the hills is so remote that it was not discovered by the outside world until the 1990s. Then, in 2006, a small group of archaeologists returned to the cave and discovered that it holds a shrine associated with rituals and sacrifices to the python, one of the region's most culturally important creatures. These findings revealed that man's sacred activities, and therefore perhaps notions of cosmology, were active about 30,000 years earlier than had been thought previously. A rock at the mouth of the cave resembles a python head, with snakeskin marks made by blows from handheld stones. On digging a trench at the foot of the rock, the archaeologists found not only the 70,000-year-old tools that had fashioned the snake head; they also found 13,000 spearheads and objects commonly used in ritual activity. None of these artefacts were of local material, but from outside the area. Furthermore, the spearheads were particularly finely crafted from colourful stone, the red ones having been burned. As there are no traces at all of domestic or other activity, scientists have concluded that the burning of the spearheads was sacrificial. Unusually for the area, this cave only holds two paintings, one of an elephant, the other a giraffe. These, together with the python, represent the three creatures historically most spiritually significant to the locality. Art and sacred space have a time-honoured bond.

left It is astonishing that these rock paintings have survived exposure to the elements in the harsh environment of the Kalahari Desert. Yet art and nature are here hand in hand and speak to the spirit as they always have. The name Kalahari means a 'waterless place', though as we can see from the vegetation, seasonal rain brings life-supporting verdure.

The Stone Circles of Senegambia
Gambia and Senegal

The Saloum and Gambia rivers border an area encompassing the mysterious stone circles of Senegambia. The high concentration of ancient stone circles here is truly unique. The rings, set in four groups along a 350-kilometre (218-mile) stretch of the River Gambia, divulge little about their function or their makers, except that they are grave markers. What is known is that they were built and used between the third century BC and the sixteenth century AD. Although no longer used in a formal fashion, the circles are traditionally visited and honoured with fruits and small stones that are said to glow at night. The circles and numerous burial mounds relate that the dead were brought here, ceremonially, on their last corporal journey before departing to the next world.

The stones themselves are mainly cylindrical, though some are square-sided or tapered and others have cupped hollows or spheres formed in their tops. The height varies from ring to ring, yet within each circle the height is largely consistent, with the tallest stone measuring 2 metres (6½ feet). Small in comparison to European stone circles, these ones are up to 6 metres (20 feet) in diameter with a maximum number of 14 stones. The pillars are cut from laterite, which is easy to quarry yet hardens on exposure to air. Having been fashioned to a sophisticated degree by iron tools, their manufacture indicates an organized society with sufficient stability to allocate the time needed to craft these things with care, respect and a clearly long-term plan. Implicit in this is a love and attentiveness to the departeds' future needs as they move on to the next life. Grave goods deal with identity and sustenance – a circlet on the wrist, a weapon (often a spear) and some pottery, usually inverted. These are of the type still made and used by local people today.

While stone circles elsewhere indicate calendrical functions, there is nothing here to suggest astronomical alignments. Rather, a different language may be contained within the rings. The late Islamic scholar, Alhaji Kemoring Jaiteh, explained that the close positioning of two stones, one large and one small, marked a parent and child burial. And he suggests that V-shaped stones mark the shared grave of two relatives who died on the same day.

But what of the circular formation? Symbolically, a circle almost universally represents harmony, the absolute and perfection. This in turn implies heaven and eternity; within the world of magic and healing, the circle is protective against demons. Futhermore, circumambulation at sacred sites is widespread, taking the form of processions and micro-pilgrimage. To walk a ceremonial circle is to follow the path of the sun, stars and planets and consolidates the cosmic link between heaven and earth. It is speculative, but not unrealistic, to suggest that these circles formed processional paths connected with the funerary function. In recent years, a museum has opened at the Gambian (Wassau) site to try to solve the mystery of these intriguing stones, and to share existing knowledge with the hundreds of scientists and tourists who visit each year in their quest for knowledge and understanding.

left The mysterious stone circles at Wassau hold many secrets, and therefore tempt the imagination. Unlike European stone circles, these ones seem to have no calendrical function, although they do honour the dead and hold a hidden language in their shapes and positioning.

right The stone circles in this region number about 1,000 and were erected over a long period of time. They are by no means fully understood, but research continues to uncover, bit by bit, some of their mysteries and secrets. It is now thought that there may be some geometric pattern linking the sites of many of the circles.

The Qumran Caves
Judean Desert, Israel

The Qumran Caves are located in the Judean Desert, which lies between the mountains of Judea in the west and the Dead Sea to the east. It was here that an amazing discovery was made in 1947. A young Bedouin shepherd, whether looking for one of his flock, for shade from the sun, or simply drawn by natural curiosity, was drawn to explore one particular cave. What he found there stunned the world. For his discovery brought to light some highly important documents. Within storage jars were delicate and extensive parchment scrolls, written in an ancient hand. On sharing the discovery with friends, one of them recognized the script as resembling the Syriac Aramaic that he had seen in a church in Bethlehem. The shepherds took some of the scrolls to the Syrian Monastery in Bethlehem and from there they were passed to the library of the central monastery in Jerusalem. Eventually, they were found to date from the beginning of the Christian era and were purchased during 1954 for safekeeping. Further exploration by Bedouins and archaeologists found yet more manuscripts in 11 caves. Dating from the third century BC to the first century AD, they are collectively know as the Dead Sea Scrolls. From these fragile fragments of parchment and papyrus, around 850 manuscripts have been reassembled, the texts being Hebrew, Aramaic and Greek.

right The discovery of a library of scrolls preserved in jars in the Qumran Caves was entirely serendipitous. It opened up new understandings of life from around the dawn of Christianity and the texts show that the biblical translations we know today are reassuringly accurate. There is little difference between the trusted tenth-century translation of Isaiah and the ancient scroll.

below More than 200 fragments of the Dead Sea Scrolls are kept safely in the Shrine of the Book in Jerusalem. Among them is this, the Isaiah Scroll. It holds the entire book of Isaiah, which is translated and present in modern-day Bibles. It represents an astonishing seed of sacred word which has journeyed into many homes, hearts and holy buildings down the ages.

The manuscripts, many of which can now be seen at the Shrine of the Book at the Israel Museum in Jerusalem, vary in content but include exciting examples of the earliest known texts from the Hebrew Bible, some of which were extant only in translation, others previously unknown. Study of the scrolls has opened up new understanding of Judaism, early Christianity and social structures within the period they cover. It is generally thought that these finds were the library of the sect who inhabited Qumran, who had chosen to remove themselves from the temptations of the city to the purity of the desert and to live by their own solar calendar and refined rules. This is the land of the biblical wilderness, where John the Baptist preached repentance and the coming of the Messiah, living on locusts and wild honey. It is the place at which Jesus was baptized in the River Jordan and to where he withdrew for 40 days, facing temptation by the Devil. It was sparsely populated, mountainous and difficult to farm, though not as dry as we see it today, and forested in places. The land has been continually used for grazing, hence the shepherd's journey into the cave and his discovery of those scrolls. Planted like seeds of knowledge, they lay dormant and were brought to blossom in the light of skilful translation. Today, pilgrims may visit them in the museum in Jerusalem. Or they may choose to immerse themselves in wilderness sites such as Qumran, the ancient monasteries, or the baptismal waters of the River Jordan, or simply camp under the stars to meditate upon what this astonishing landscape has witnessed.

right This is cave four, which yielded the largest number of finds, though as they were not in jars their condition was fragile. More than 15,000 fragments and 122 biblical scrolls or part scrolls were found here. However, no New Testament scrolls have ever been found.

below It is said that the shepherd who first discovered the Dead Sea Scrolls took his friends to explore the caves and found more documents. These they hung from their tents, including the Isaiah Scroll and the Thanksgiving Psalm Scroll.

The Findhorn Foundation
Moray Firth, Scotland

The Moray Firth enjoys more than 800 kilometres (500 miles) of varied coastline in northeast Scotland. Many smaller estuaries run to join it, passing cliffs and sandy beaches on their way to the North Sea and offering a haven for the wildlife that frequent these waters. The Findhorn Foundation was founded in 1962, almost inadvertently, by Peter and Eileen Caddy, their three young sons and friend Dorothy Maclean. When Peter dug a kitchen garden in the grounds of the caravan park where they lived, he could never have imagined that he was planting the roots of a new spiritual community; or that the growth of both garden and group would be nurtured by Dorothy's innate understanding of the plants' intrinsic needs and Eileen's spiritual wisdom, channelled through intense meditation. Yet the succulent abundance that thrived in the dry salty ground drew the attention of the outside world and the garden became a source of inspiration for many. It was not long before the group's conviction and lifestyle drew others who sought to follow their example, and a community was born.

By the late 1960s Eileen was publishing her spiritual insights and guidance through the newly established Findhorn Press. These writings reached and moved such large numbers of people that the foundation had to expand into new dwellings, workshops and communal rooms. By the 1970s, the community was committed to new ways of sustainable living which foster peaceful relationships and self knowledge, along with inner listening and co-creation with nature; these principles stand firm today, in what is now an exemplary eco village, an educational centre and a place of alternative healing. As with other religious communities, concern for, and service to, the world beyond its walls is paramount. Members have forged links with other organizations, such as the United Nations, opening outwards to share experience, learning and knowledge for the benefit of future generations.

No single faith is prioritized at Findhorn. Instead, spiritual balance and growth are at the core of exploring and learning from all the world's religions. Today the foundation embraces several hundred people who live on site or who have settled nearby. Thousands of visitors come each year from across the world to take part, help and nurture their inner health through meditation, the educational programme and workshops.

right The Moray Firth is the largest firth in Scotland, its name in Gaelic being *An Cuan Moireach*. It is an important home for the harbour porpoise and, interestingly, the bottlenose dolphin, used in art as a spirit guide, leading souls to safety.

ROUTES AND REASONS

The route of a sacred journey is the road from yesterday that stretches to tomorrow. It is the passage that allows our faults, failures and problems to fall away as we approach a future in which sins have been forgiven, inner peace restored and blessings sought. Early on in the history of faith we learn of an awareness of the spirit by place, water, cave or mountain top, points where energies collect or emanate and where heaven seems to brush us with its breath.

left Shatrunjaya Mountain in Gujarat is studded with Jain temples. These are holy shrines on sacred soil – a smudge of earth from the mountain is meant to destroy sin and free the faithful's soul. Pilgrims climb 3,950 steps to reach the top, a steep ascent that takes 90 minutes, but which is rewarded by exuberant art.

These natural landscapes are often the places where we find spiritual benefit. Just as the pounding of waves upon a beach can invigorate and refresh us, so we notice how a cascade slowly reshapes all it touches, as it spills from one level to the next. There is a sense of excitement and power in the sounds and sight of water as it changes speed and outline, transforming from smooth surface to spume and spray.

Wherever we are in the landscape, be it urban or rural, sunshine brings sparkling clarity while mist and dusk may excite our sense of mystery or chill us with foreboding. The elements and seasons affect our feelings and, if we let them in, these can be the triggers of heightened perception, those inspirations that make us stop to consider the world and all that it contains. These are good enough reasons in themselves to set off to the coast, the countryside or a park, where we can connect with creation and feel the joy of colour, scent and scene. And those are the presences long recognized by people who sense the maker in all that is, the spirit within every last cell and atom of nature, and so sacredness makes its presence felt.

There are many reasons to embark upon a pilgrimage, such as the need to express penitence, make intercession, for healing, or to seek or give thanks for blessings, and the journey is often made to a site associated with a particular event or a key figure.

In the icy Canadian Arctic Archipelago, the Inuit built their Inuksuit rock formations for practical reasons, as navigational markers in a land where detail and direction are obscured by low light and driving snow. As such these rocky cairns became lifelines and took on tutelary status. In many cases they have been sited where the landscape holds some force, perhaps danger, and they may have been a source of refuge and comfort – a place for the traveller to draw strength and lift his or her mood before moving on. The purpose of the Inuit journeys was often hunting, which needed negotiation with the spirit world for endurance, success and safe return.

In the Hindu faith, Saint Sambandar journeyed through the world with joyful dance steps as he healed and helped troubled souls by singing his magical *padigams* in praise to Lord Shiva.

Associated with the Meenakshi Amman temple in Madurai, India, he allowed his natural exuberance to lift other people's sickness and transform it into health, and untangled problems to smooth the way forward.

Events, such as religious apparitions or the birthplaces of the sacred, are often reasons for travel. On Shikoku Island, 88 places connected to Kūkai, the 'great saint who spreads the teaching', are linked by a pilgrimage on foot. Those who follow that path do so in the belief that Kūkai is still there, in the temples and along the route, and their staffs and packs bear words to that effect. In the woods near a village in the Czech Republic, an angelic vision experienced by an ordinary man gave rise to his family's healing, and precipitated the ongoing international Pilgrimage of Reconciliation, while the Hejnice cathedral there draws those needing spiritual rest and restoration. On the island of Tinos in Greece, dreams associated with the Virgin Mary led to an ancient figure of her being found in a field. Thus a humble plot took on sacred resonance, and became a point to which pilgrims now come, many by boat; after disembarking,

some make the last part of the journey on their hands and knees. They come in penitence to seek forgiveness, healing or fertility. This hands-and-knees journey covers a relatively short distance and takes about an hour. For most people, that trip taken on foot would be little more than an interesting saunter. The discomfort and self-abasement are an endurance test, forcing the pilgrim into a particular frame of mind, one of humility, perhaps, or alignment with the suffering of another.

Similarly, those who visit the Palitana temples on Shatrunjaya Mountain must refrain from eating and drinking, regardless of the arduous climb. Sacrificing comfort brings an awareness of the importance of the pilgrimage and prepares the mind for its resonance, demonstrating commitment and the significance of the process. Where sacredness asserts its presence, ways to reach and grow in it will be found.

below left to right Baffin Island, Canada – the site of many Inuksuk; Shikoku temple, Shikoku Island, Japan; Ramu Setu (Adam's Bridge), Plait Strait, Sri Lanka and India; Le Morne Brabant, Mauritius.

Inuksuit
Baffin Island, Canada

The Arctic hosts the extremes of nature, which cannot fail to fire the imagination: the bitter cold, the midnight sun and the polar night. The region is under the Ursa Major, the crowning constellation of the Great Bear which lights the clear night sky; a display so beautiful, yet which can be outshone by the glory of the Aurora Borealis. These natural phenomena are just some of the enchanting elements that inform the Inuit culture. Within the landscape are Inuksuit, manmade stone structures built to mark a route or a significant site in a place that is largely devoid of natural landmarks. Varying in shape and size, they are helpful markers to travellers and have become woven into the legends of the Arctic region. And so the Inuksuit straddle the outer world of pragmatism and the inner realm of mythology.

Featuring in the canon of Inuit tales is the story of Kiviuq, the intrepid legendary traveller and Inuit folk hero. His journeys are in the realm of myth and the spirit, yet set in a landscape that is very real and which is interpreted by the Inuit according to their cultural heritage and their centuries-old associations. Kiviuq is an intrepid mythical character who

wanders through time and space, grappling with beings from the physical and metaphysical worlds. These shape-shifters display the spectrum of human weakness – jealousy, greed and cruelty; and it is Kiviuq's task to outwit and escape them. He sometimes travels by earthly means, with the help of birds or animals, or by singing, for Kiviuq is a shaman. A shaman will use his powers to help others, often through healing, and any who abuse their potency will always suffer the consequences.

left The Inuit sense the power of the Arctic wilderness and celebrate it in their culture. But landscape here may be veiled by the shifting elements and power points need marking. An Inuksuk built of stones can pinpoint the spiritual in a landscape by heralding a threshold and acting as a reassuring presence.

below The term Inuksuk means 'to represent a human presence', and while some are made to stand out in the landscape and act as route markers, others are discreetly placed and invite more intimate appreciation. Each is unique and built to achieve balance in a hostile environment.

Although Kiviuq has many supernatural qualities, he has human vulnerabilities too, and within the Inuit tradition it is customary to relate both his weaknesses and strengths. To many of the Inuit, Kiviuq is a prophet and his stories act as guidance, his strengths to be emulated and his mistakes to be learned from. The listener must distinguish the good from the bad and act accordingly, choosing which part of the action to mirror and which to turn away from.

One story involving Kiviuq begins with an orphan boy who lived with his grandmother. He was tormented by others in the community; repeatedly they tore his clothes and made his life a misery. Eventually the grandmother decided to take revenge by turning the child into a seal, which lured the miscreants out to sea in their kayaks. A storm was invoked to capsize the vessels and drown the tormentors. Kiviuq, who had not joined in with the cruelty, was spared, by virtue of his kindness, his shamanic skills and the help of his guardian spirits. He goes on to receive warnings and advice from Inuksuit on the shore, as he paddles his kayak dangerously close to giant clams.

The mythologies are a source of wisdom handed down to steer future generations through the difficulties of living in this often hostile environment. And while guidance is epitomized and contained within the Inuksuit, the character of Kiviuq becomes something of a symbolic Inuksuit, by his presence in the cultural landscape of lore.

right above The Arctic winters are dark, and regions north of the Arctic Circle experience days without any sun. The sun sets in late November and remains out of sight until mid January. By contrast, the daylight can last for 24 hours during the summer, and there are more days of this, the midnight sun, close to the North Pole.

right below Here on Baffin Island, shifting light and low cloud create an eerie atmosphere that is met by the sounds of howling wind. Sun bounces off the snow, spilling luminous colour and sharp shadows in a magical display across the sharply ridged and furrowed peaks. The mountains are over 2,440 metres (8,005 feet) high and hold untold mysteries, for few venture far.

below An Inuit man on Baffin Island's Admiralty Inlet, in Nunavut, rests his dogs and contemplates the sky. Nunavut means 'our land' in the Inuit tongue, which indicates the bond between man and place. Natural forces shape the landscape and dictate how people may live here. Winter temperatures average -32°C (-25°F) on Baffin Island, so all life forms have adapted accordingly.

Meenakshi Amman Temple

Madurai, Tamil Nadu, India

It is said that a *padigam* (song) is a garland of ten verses to the glory of God, and devotion the thread on which the flowers of verse are strung. Flowers are a recurring theme in Madurai. Famous for its sweet-smelling jasmine, the city's original ground plan resembles a lotus flower and it is named after the divine nectar, or *madhu*, that fell from Lord Shiva's hair as he blessed the place and its people.

One of the saints associated with this city, and instrumental in its devotion to Shaivism, is the seventh-century Sambandar, a young musician famous for singing and composing miraculous *padigams*. His devotional life began when he was three years old, with a vision of Lord Shiva and the goddess Parvati who gave him golden cymbals and milk respectively. The infant responded with a song of his own composition, singing and dancing for the rest of his short life. Though Sambandar's

journey through life was taken in dance steps, it was not one of frivolity. He undertook a life of pilgrimage in honour of Lord Shiva, which led him far across the south of India, performing his miraculous songs which

right The temple complex includes 12 extraordinary *gopurams*. These are tall, tapering towers that grace the entrance to the temple. Here, painted sculptures jostle for space across the walls. Gods and goddesses, beasts and demons stand on ledges and peep out beneath the feet of the figures above.

below The Golden Lotus Pond, or Potramarai Kulam, holds holy water accessible by steps, so that pilgrims may bathe. The pool is older than the temple and was noted for the poets and scholars, including the Tamil Sangam, who were inspired to gather and debate around its banks.

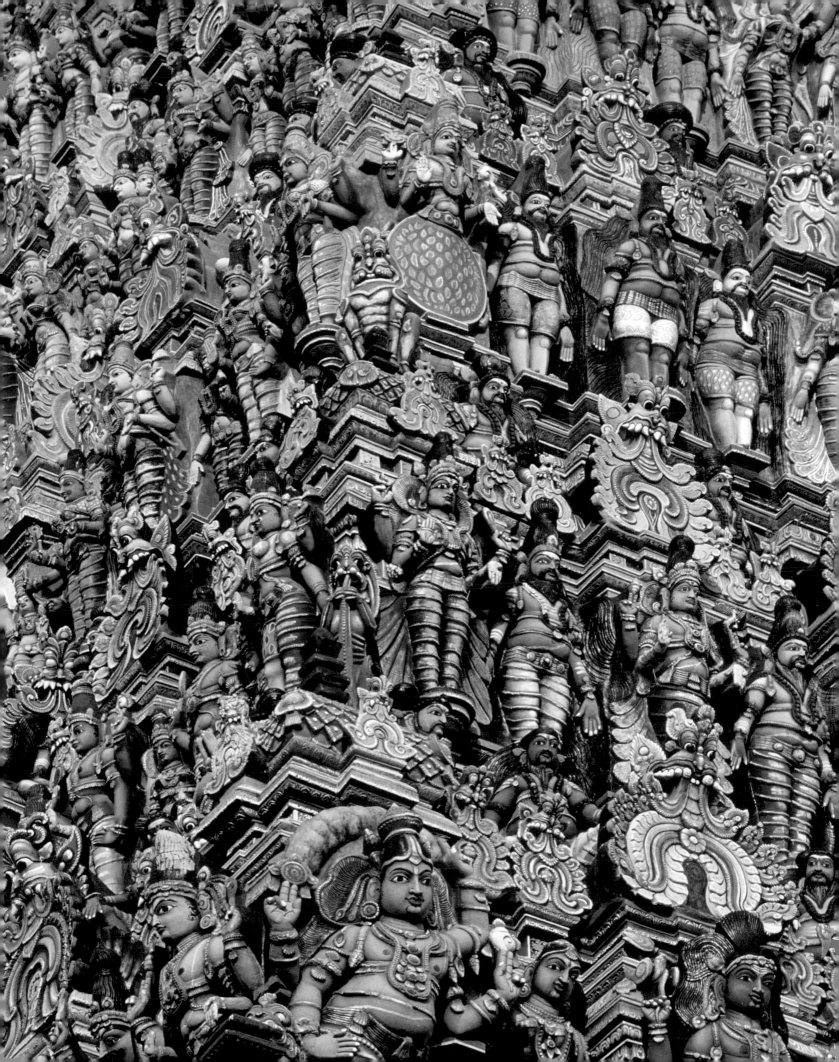

could heal illness, awaken the dead and cure suffering. Along the way he was summoned to Madurai to help the queen, who was unable to practice devotion to Shiva for fear of the king's allegiance to Jainism, which had all but wiped out Shaivism. There then followed a series of contests between Sambandar and the Jains, involving a fire that was set by the Jains. Sambandar quenched the fire with a *padigam* but it returned and infected the king with a burning illness. This Sambandar cured with holy ash. Next, it was agreed that the written words of Shaivism and Jainism should undergo tests of fire and of water. When the Jains' first words were consumed by fire and the second set was washed away by the river, Sambandar's written *padigams* survived the licking flames and swam upstream to safety. At this, the Jains admitted defeat, and the king and his people returned to Shaivism.

And so a place of worship was built. The temple is dedicated to Lord Shiva and Parvati in their forms as Sundareswarar and Meenakshi. It stands at the heart of this 2,500-year-old city, which has a sacred ground plan honouring the four cardinal points and through them reaches out to the cosmos. The temple complex includes 12 sumptuously decorated *gopurams* (towers), and the sacred pond, the Potramarai Kulam, which is circumambulated before entering the shrine. The Thousand Pillar Hall is here, too, with its exquisitely carved columns, each one unique and, appropriately, some are musical and release different notes when struck. The temple is a place of repeated celebration, with many festivals taking place throughout the year, the most important one marking the divine marriage of Sundareswarar and Meenakshi. Sambandar's *padigams* echo down the centuries and resound from the walls here; they are still sung and form start of the Tamil Shaivite canon of hymns devoted to Shiva.

left This image gives some idea of the scale of the temple complex and the degree of craftsmanship that has gone into its making. The craftworkers know that the divine is present in the stone, and it is their job to reveal that presence through their skill.

above right The Sanctuary of the Golden Dome stands beside the North *gopuram*, which has nine storeys and is nearly 50 metres (164 feet) tall. The stucco figures on the *gopurams* are repaired and repainted every 12 years.

right A pilgrim stands in prayer beneath the cloister, which skirts the Golden Lotus Pond, taking a quiet moment away from the throng. It is traditional to circumnavigate the pond before entering the temple, which is visited by 6,000 people on normal days and countless more at festival times.

overleaf Fabulous columns and carvings fill the Thousand Pillar Hall. When struck, each pillar chimes with a different note, as if the beasts portrayed are singing *padigams* and praise.

The Palitana Temples
Palitana, Gujarat, India

The city of Palitana can trace its first ruler, Thakur Sahib Sejaki, back to 1194. By that time, Jain temple-building had already been going on for around a century. Given that Jainism dates to the sixth century BC, it is likely that pilgrimage and ritual took place well before these architectural roots were planted. The first Tirthankar, (a human being who achieves enlightenment through asceticism and love for others, and becomes a spiritual teacher), Lord Adinath (Rishabha), is said to have attained infinite knowledge here; so clearly Palitana has an ancient association with Jainism. It was Adinath – the name means 'most excellent' – who taught the skills of husbandry, farming and domestic life. Furthermore, it is said that he had sufficient insight to be able to recognize the given aptitudes in any individual and taught them arts, crafts, languages or martial arts according to their natural inclinations.

It is the close association with this charismatic figure that has led to Palitana becoming Jainism's most important pilgrim destination. It is a place of auspicious splendour and has witnessed the salvation of countless souls inspired by the example of Lord Adinath and his 99 visits here. Often called the pilgrimage of all pilgrimages, there are now 863 temples spreading from the base to the two peaks of Shatrunjaya Mountain. The main road through the city is lined with shrines, resting places and charitable boarding houses offering accommodation to travellers. However, the pilgrimage itself begins at the foot of the mountain and preferably after bathing in the Shatrunjay River. The arduous route to the top is a steep 3.5 kilometre (2¼ mile) ascent up 3,950 steps, and the climb takes an average of 90 minutes. The very substance of the mountain itself is regarded as being vibrantly sacred, to the extent that a smudge of its soil on the head of a pilgrim is sufficient to destroy sin and wipe away worldly concerns. For those who find the slope too much, there is a model of the mountain that may be venerated instead, though it is customary to call at no less than five temples during the pilgrimage. The splendour of the marble temples, the carvings, sculptures and sacred spaces transport the journey into the realm of visual wonder; and also awe for the labourers who toiled with the weight of heavy materials and for the craftspeople whose work has

left Pattern, rhythm and repetition enter through the eye and into the soul, lifting the pilgrim out of daily existence into a new consciousness. The route up the Shatrunjaya Mountain leads pilgrims into any of the 863 temples and shrines here, but all must leave before nightfall, as the gods need quiet.

above The architects who visualized and designed the temples knew how to create a sense of presence. Symmetry, proportion and perspective are all used to lead the eye and envelop the pilgrim in a welcoming harmony.

right Today's pilgrims visit the temple complex to seek healing, spiritual cleansing and uplift, or in some cases to ask for fertility. At one shrine, it is traditional for women to leave tiny cradles in the hope of conceiving a child.

delighted so many. Despite the climb and the energy it demands, pilgrims must abstain from eating or even carrying food, out of respect for the sanctity of this mountain of the gods. Everyone must be ready to descend from the mountain at dusk, as at night the deities are to be left in peace; tomorrow will bring a fresh wave of pilgrims and the cycle of burning incense, chanting, and bell ringing will begin again, aspiring to right faith, right knowledge and right conduct.

above In the foreground, a man sweeps the marble floor in front of the temple clear of insects for fear of causing harm; *ahimsa*, or non-injury, is one of the Jain monks' vows.

above Being surrounded by beautiful architecture is akin to being in a
harmonious landscape. All things have been considered and refined, and a
balance exists between component parts, each making space for its neighbour.

Kumbh Mela
Allahabad, Uttar Pradesh, India

Prayag (meaning 'place of sacrifice') is believed to be the place at which Brahma first made oblations after creating the world. It is the ancient name for the city otherwise known, since 1583, as Allahabad. For Hindus this is a site of tremendous spiritual significance. Thousands of years ago the gods and demons agreed to work together to churn *amrit* (nectar) from the primordial milky ocean and to take equal shares of the resulting elixir. However, when the precious pot, or *kumbha*, appeared, brimming with *amrit*, the demons snatched it from the ocean and ran away. The gods, of course, pursued them and a battle followed, a fight which lasted for 12 nights and days – 12 years in earthly terms. The *amrit* spilt and splashed to earth, landing in Nashik, Ujjain, Haridwar and Prayag; these four sacred spills became the sites of cyclical pilgrimage for Kumbh Mela celebrations, which have taken place for thousands of years since that sky-borne battle.

Once in the 12-year cycle the greatest celebration, the Maha Kumbh Mela, occurs at Prayag. Drawing around 60 million people, it is the biggest gathering on earth. But Prayag enjoys yet more sanctity, standing as it does at the triple confluence, or Triveni Sangam, of the sacred rivers Ganges, Yamuna and the mystical Sarasvati. The dates of the Kumbh Mela are calculated through astronomy, the Maha Kumbh Mela being held when Jupiter is in Aquarius (known in India as the Kumbh) and the Sun and Moon are in Capricorn.

below The three sacred rivers – the Ganges, the Yamuna and the Sarasvati – meet here at Prayag, making this place thrice blessed. The year 2001 saw the largest human gathering ever recorded; this was a Maha Kumbh Mela at the end of a 144-year cycle. The heavenly bodies formed alignments not seen in all of those years, as if to mark the turning of a new millenium. It is estimated that around 70 million people gathered here: the combination of sacred time and sacred place made attendance highly propitious.

right Here a procession crosses a pontoon bridge – the river is an artery of faith throughout India, ever flowing yet ever present. When the pilgrims enter the mass centre, they do so in a line, holding onto the ends of clothes.

left The fifth day of Maha Kumbh Mela celebrations sees the start of spring; this is a time to wear yellow and pray for bountiful harvests.

below For Hindus, to wear yellow, which comes from turmeric, is to celebrate spring. It is the colour of happiness and meditation, because it is mentally stimulating. Here it is combined with saffron, which is the tint of purity through the cleansing effects of fire. It also indicates abstinence and rejection of worldly concerns in the quest for light.

Within the 42-day festival, some days are more auspicious for bathing than others, and at these times the celestial nexus gives the waters the supreme ability to absolve bathers from their sins. Gratitude for this cleansing is sufficient to wash away any practical concerns about the cleanliness of the water, crowding, personal comfort and so on. People from all walks of life share in the experience, basking in the joy of the festival and the closeness to God that it allows. The weak are helped into the water by the strong, and in allowing that closeness the weak help the strong. Personal devotions take the form of prayer, chanting, meditation, acts of charity and sacrifice. The concentration of monks, saints, sadhus, yogis and everyone's devout activity feeds the sanctity of the event, increasing its authority and potency. Some of these holy people spend most of their lives apart from the rest of society, only leaving their solitude once in 12 years for this great gathering. Their blessing, or *darshan*, is a rare privilege for those who receive it. The Procession of Holy Saints is another source of powerful *shakti*, or sacred energy. This is a colourful and noisy event with the holy people moving along by horse, palanquin, elephant or camel – the variety of transport, clothing, lack of clothing and personal charisma represents the spectrum of faith traditions and the diversity celebrated here. Many may feel overwhelmed by the visual and acoustic intensity of the event, but faith is the great sustainer.

Shikoku Pilgrimage
Shikoku Island, Japan

Shikoku is the smallest of Japan's four main islands, being 225 kilometres (140 miles) long and up to 150 kilometres (93 miles) wide. It lies tucked into the space left by Honshu and Kyushu islands, to the east of where they almost touch. All around the island, mostly towards the coastline, are sprinkled the 88 temples that collectively make up the Shikoku pilgrim route. Between them they will take you up mountains and through forests, along beaches and roads, though rain and into strong winds. And to understand why this pilgrimage visits so many places requires an introduction to Kūkai, who was born in AD 774 with the name Saeki no Mao.

As a boy, Kūkai showed great educational promise and was directed towards a high-powered career, but he never felt inspired by what was expected of him and sought a deeper calling. On meeting a Buddhist monk, he learned the art of meditation, began to see the virtues of the priesthood and left university. He studied Buddhist texts and spent long periods alone, deep in meditation within a cave at the south of the island, gazing upon nothing but the heavens and the ocean. He took the name Kūkai, which means Sky and Sea, in honour of his life-changing decision to become a monk and shunned the material trappings of everyday life in favour of poverty and learning. Wanting to extend his knowledge of Buddhism, he became frustrated by the lack of Buddhist teachers in Japan and eventually found his way to China. There, Abbot Hui-Kuo, seventh patriarch of Esoteric Buddhism, recognized Kūkai as having an exceptional understanding, and after only three months of study Kūkai was ordained as the Abbot's successor and instructed by him to return home at the earliest opportunity, to spread the teachings, which he did.

On his return to Japan in AD 806, Kūkai had with him more than 450 scrolls of scripture and *sutras*, along with ceremonial images and objects. Kūkai's reputation as a teacher grew and he wrote extensively on Esoteric and Exoteric Buddhism, oversaw the building

left The pilgrimage is a well-trodden route and to walk the whole way takes two to three months. The pilgrims are called Henro, or O-Henro-San. Their white garments are death robes, and traditionally if a Henro dies during the journey, his walking staff, which represents Kūkai (Kobo Daishi) and is inscribed with the words 'Daishi and I going together', becomes his grave post.

right Traditionally, the walk is made clockwise, visiting each of the 88 temples in turn. However, one of Kūkai's contemporaries deliberately walked the other way so as to be sure of meeting the sage, and some Henro follow that idea. It is traditional to stop at each temple as the number 88 represents all the sins known in Buddhism. If each is met, all sin can be expunged.

of monasteries and firmly established Shingon Buddhism within Japanese culture. Kūkai accurately predicted the date of his own death during AD 835 and, nearly 100 years later, he was posthumously given the name Kobo Daishi, the 'great saint who spreads the teaching', by imperial order. Tales of his goodness permeated into folklore and there are hundreds of stories about his miracles and healing, which partly account for the affection in which he is still held. His followers took to visiting the places associated with his life and ministry, and this is thought to be the origin of the Shikoku pilgrimage. Some say that the 88 temples equal the number of evil passions identified by certain branches of Buddhism, and that by visiting the temples those passions can be conquered. Pilgrims carry a staff bearing the legend 'Daishi and I going together', bearing witness to the fact that he is considered to be still very much alive and a supportive companion along the way.

left Ishite Ji Temple is one of the most popular temples. It is a three-storey pagoda with fine artworks of the gods, worked in various media. The temple is overlooked by a huge stone sculpture of the Buddha, which stands amid trees. It is traditional to strike the temple bells on arrival to alert the deities of their guests' arrival.

left below Pilgrims carry official *osamefuda* name cards to leave at the temple; they may also be given to people who offer help along the way. The cards are colour-coded according to the number of pilgrimages made. Gold is the colour for those who have walked more than 30 times. Many pilgrims take scrolls or albums to be inscribed and stamped with the temple seal.

right Not many of today's pilgrims can afford the length of time it takes to walk the full pilgrimage, so take at least part of the journey by other means. The important thing is to take part and to visit as many temples as possible.

Rama Setu (Adam's Bridge)
Palk Strait, Sri Lanka and India

Rama Setu is the bridge crossed by Prince Rama of Ayodhya when he sought to rescue his bride Sita from the clutches of Ravana, the demon king of Sri Lanka. This story is told in the epic tale *Ramayana*, and for centuries the existence of the bridge has stayed within the realm of myth; though said to link India with Sri Lanka, no one knew for certain where it left the mainland and touched the island's shores. However, satellite photographs taken by the space agency NASA show that a physical link does exist. A 30-kilometre (18½-mile) thread of reef shoals lies just below the shallow waters between the Gulf of Mannar and the Palk Strait, in a sinuous line that is clearly discernible yet discovered only by accident.

The *Ramayana*, attributed to the poet Valmiki, was written around 400 BC. It is a tale of two brothers, Rama and Lakshmana, whose rescue mission leads them to travel the length of India, facing danger, demons and difficulties, while also helping the weak and needy. However, looking beyond the daring adventures and kindly deeds we see a metaphor for godly behaviour. Rama is an incarnation of Vishnu, the embodiment of goodness and virtue, and this venture is an example of how to conquer difficulties through steadfast faith. As the story progresses it also demonstrates that resolve and determination are necessary tools for keeping to the right path. Furthermore, it illustrates the value of accepting help and working with others, for each has a part to play and unique gifts to offer, contributing selflessly of their best. For although Rama sets out on this journey with only his brother, they are eventually helped by an army of monkeys and by Hanuman, the monkey god. Hanuman leaps across the sea to Lanka and discovers the place in which Sita is held, reassures her and then goes back to assist Rama. Together they build the bridge, conquer the demon Ravana and return home. Rama and Sita's troubles don't end there, but they have crossed a physical and metaphorical bridge and their life continues.

The discovery of the Rama Setu was a great joy to the Hindu community; it exposed a tangible link with ancient mythology and represents a connection with Rama himself. However, once it was seen and mapped it also represented a breachable barrier. Breaking the bridge to allow passage for large vessels has been a highly controversial proposition, not only cutting across the sacred Rama Setu but also severing a new-found connection for those who treasure its existence and symbolism. Hindus are supported in their protests against the project by environmentalists who know the Gulf of Mannar to be one of Asia's most splendid coastal regions, and sensitive to disruption. Whatever the outcome of this twenty-first-century battle, Lord Rama will always be known as a bringer of peace and righteousness; his birth is celebrated in one of the most important Hindu festivals, the Sri-Ramnavami.

right It used to be thought that the physical link between India and Sri Lanka existed only in mythology. But as this photograph taken from the space shuttle *Discovery* shows, there is such a link. The reef shoals touch from island to mainland like outstretched fingers. In Hindu mythology, this bridge has existed for thousands of years but kept itself hidden from man.

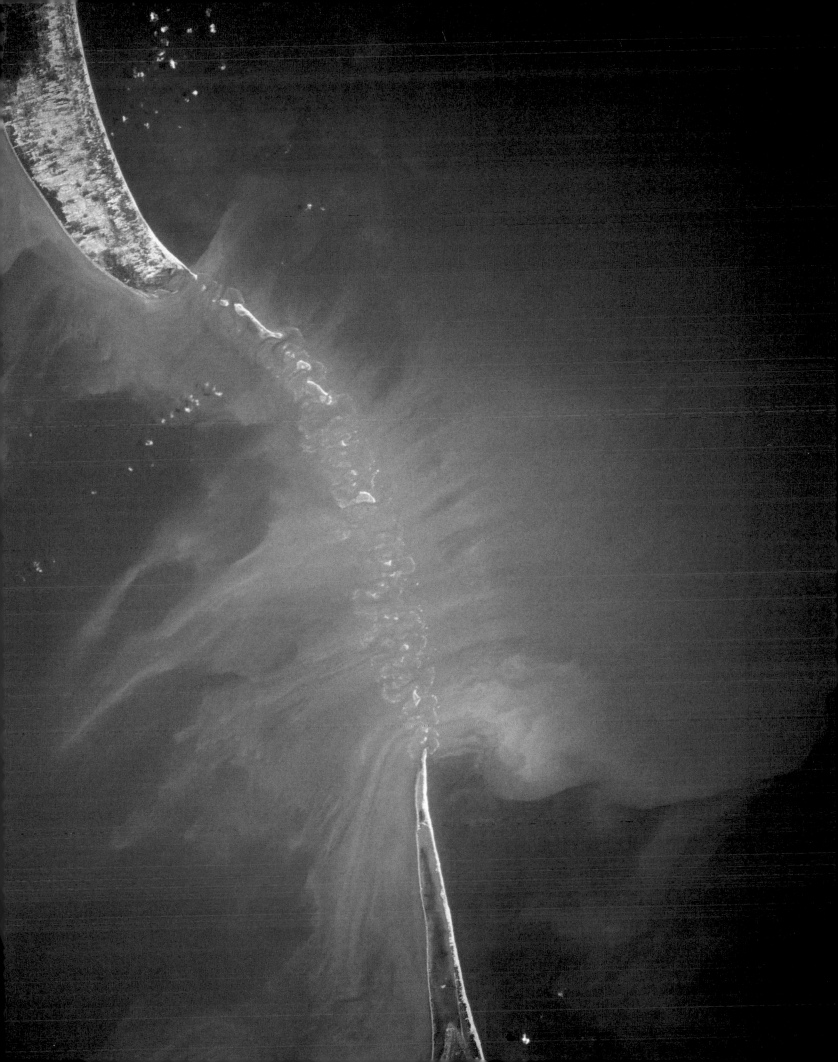

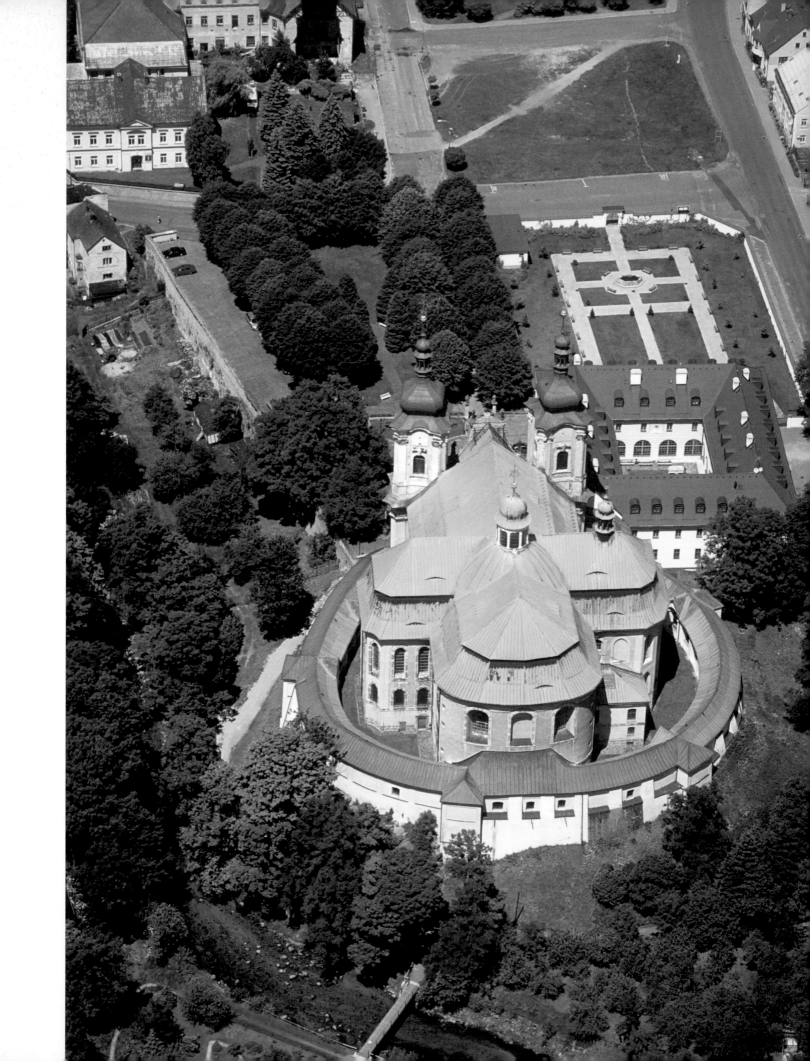

Czech Mariazell
Hejnice, Czech Republic

Where the Czech Republic meets Poland and Germany, the Jizerské Mountains give way to a valley that once was home to ancient woodland. The sacred journey to the international pilgrim site that evolved here has its humble roots within those woods. It is said that a poor workman left his sickly wife and daughter at home while he went to collect firewood. Exhausted by the work, he took rest beneath the fragrant branches of a linden tree, a species hallowed in Eastern Europe for absorbing people's sicknesses and repelling lightning. As he rested, the man had a vision of the tree illuminated by the glory of two angels in its branches, who told him that the place was favoured by God and must be adorned with an image of the Virgin Mary, so that those who passed might obtain a blessing. So the man went to the village and bought a small carving as described and lodged it in the tree. He then fetched his wife and daughter and the family prayed together. They were overjoyed to find that they were healed and they shared their delight with all of their neighbours. Of course the good news spread, and pilgrims came to offer praise to God and to bring their own troubles in the hope that they too might be healed. The site, known as Czech Mariazell, was consecrated with a small wooden chapel, built during 1211.

In time, the number of pilgrims outgrew the original structure and it was replaced during the fifteenth century with a Gothic church; a monastery was built nearby, during the seventeenth century. Journeying here through the rugged landscape and dense forest with its wild beasts and dark nights was no easy task. However pilgrims could find a useful symbolism in these dangers, by emerging from peril and reaching safety through the support of companionship and more especially through their faith. Furthermore, prayer is often focused by immediate problems and this part of the journey could be seen as useful preparation. No doubt the joy of reaching Hejnice was magnified in the light of those difficulties, conviction strengthened and spirits lifted by safe arrival. By the eighteenth century, the pilgrim numbers and the success of the site had reached such significance that the cruciform Church of the Visitation of Our Lady was built. On its high altar still stands the original linden wood sculpture of the Virgin Mary, the Christ child in one hand and an apple in the other. Over the years various difficulties have presented themselves to the community at Hejnice in the form of fire, theft, political unrest and war. However, once communism fell during 1989 the Centre of Spiritual Revival was established. The Pilgrimage of Reconciliation is celebrated annually during May, followed by the Festival of the Visitation of Mary the Virgin during July. Throughout the year there are numerous conferences, seminars and retreats aimed at spiritual healing and renewal. And while the journey here may now be less fraught with danger, the original reasons for its establishment hold fast.

left This photograph shows an aerial view of Hejnice and the Pilgrimage Church of the Visitation of Our Lady. It is now the venue for the international Pilgrimage of Reconciliation, which draws local people as well as travellers from Poland, Germany and other parts of Europe. The town is situated beneath the slopes of the Jizerské Mountains and is an area which has been inhabited since prehistory.

Apparition Hill
Medjugorje, Bosnia-Herzegovinia

During 1934 the parish of Medjugorje marked the 1,900th anniversary of the Passion of Christ by installing images of the Stations of the Cross along a path that climbs Mount Sipovac, and they changed the peak's name to Krizevac, meaning 'the mountain of the Cross'. This became a pilgrim route that is still used today, in silent prayer by those who take its crumbly, rocky path and pause to reflect at each of the stations before moving on to the cross at the top. However, total silence in this hitherto unremarkable village is now impossible as Medjugorje is the third most-visited Catholic pilgrimage site in Europe.

During 1981, on a smaller hill called Podbrdo, the Virgin Mary appeared to six young people from Medjugorje, aged between 10 and 17. She gave them messages of peace and instructions to follow Christ. And those messages and appearances did not occur just the once; on the following day the astonished children saw the Virgin again and drew close enough to talk to her. By the third day, news of these marvellous encounters had spread and several thousand people had gathered on Podbrdo. This time, the apparition lasted for about 30 minutes and on leaving the hill one of the girls, Marija, had a further experience: she saw the Virgin in front of a rainbow-coloured cross urging the villagers to live in God's peace. By the fourth day the atheist communist authorities had become interested in the proceedings and put pressure on the priest, Father Jozo Zovko, to denounce the apparitions, which he refused to do. Subsequently, the children were taken away for questioning and examination by doctors. On their return to the village they ran back through the crowds to the top of the hill and saw yet another vision. It is estimated that by the fifth day 15,000 people had arrived, hoping to share in the excitement. Once again the children were examined by doctors seeking to dismiss the visions as hallucinations, mental illness or fabrication, yet nothing of the sort could be established. The police sought to arrest the children but Father Jozo hid them in his home, having now received divine instruction to protect them. The crowds deliberately gave the police confusing messages as to the visionaries' whereabouts. For Father Jozo this represented a welcome shift in the people's attitude because those who had come as onlookers were now engaging in the events, acting more like convinced pilgrims than baffled spectators. This change became clearer when they crowded into church to worship with the priest and to pray that God would help them all to understand the meaning of the events.

In time, the authorities came to realize that these phenomena could not be controlled. In fact the apparitions continue, with one of the original children, Mirjana, still receiving messages of love and peace on the 25th day of each month; these are sent for the parish and the whole world. So Medjugorje welcomes pilgrims from far and wide who come for the exuberant joy of the festivals or for the quietness and spiritual nourishment of the everyday.

right Krizevac is known as 'the mountain of the Cross'. Prayerful people climb this stoney mountain and leave crosses, to which prayer cloths may be tied. It is a place to come to for quiet reflection away from the busy pilgrim activity below. Elsewhere in the vicinity, other crosses mark the sites at which the Virgin Mary appeared to the children of the village.

left The first of the children's apparitions appeared on June 24, 1981; 20 years later, crowds of people came to mark the anniversary in a gathering, which moved off to sites connected with the whole story. Here they gather in the square before the parish church in Medjugorje.

right above Twenty thousand people walked the twentieth anniversary pilgrimage during 2001. Here we see priests, nuns, monks and laiety walking as far as the eye can see. Within the parish there are several religious communities, including some from abroad, who now work locally – in an orphanage, a home for single mothers or the centre for disabled children. Spiritual and practical needs are cared for in this supportive environment.

right below In the foreground of this picture we can see walkers climbing Apparition Hill; beyond them, at the figure of Our Lady, the Virgin Mary, pilgrims stop to consecrate themselves. The going is tough underfoot, so this climb is a rocky one. However, such matters are of little consequence. The journey is not about physical comfort, but spiritual growth and aligning oneself with the divine.

Bujagali Falls
Jingja, Uganda

The kingdom of Busoga is effectively an island, being skirted by Lake Kyoga and Lake Victoria, along with the rivers Nile and Mpologoma. Inevitably, water has played a huge cultural and practical role in the lives of the Busoga people. This is the story of a recent journey taken by the spirits of a sacred waterfall, who agreed to relocate for the benefit of those who lived nearby.

Below Lake Victoria the waters cascade down a series of broad steps and begin their three-month journey north to the Mediterranean Sea. The first wide drop the waters come to is called the Bujagali Falls, or *Budhagali* in the Busoga tongue. The people have known this site to be the traditional home of the spirit of Bujabald, which is embodied in a local man known as Jaja Bujabald or the Bujagali doctor. It is his job to protect the welfare of the community through ritual and healing, using local herbs and the traditions handed down to him through generations of his predecessors. The current doctor is the 39th embodiment of the Bujagali spirit and he is said to be able to exercise supernatural powers such as crossing the falls where others wouldn't dream of trying. However, he has faced a crisis that his ancestors could never have dreamed of.

Due to Uganda's shortage of energy, a new dam is to be built to generate hydroelectric power, flooding the spirits' home and the place at which they have been worshipped through the ages. The roar of the falls will be stilled as the volume of water backs up and levels out ahead of the dam, which is destined to control the spill and take its energy to homes and industries. According to the Bujagali doctor, the spirits should never be disturbed and to build the dam without appeasing them would invite disaster. However, a pragmatic solution has been found by Nfuudu, another healer, who prepared a new home for the spirits in the village of Namizzi, 8 kilometres (5 miles) along the River Nile. Nfuudu wrapped a spear, the symbol of power and defence, in a cloth of bark and left it in the pounding falls. Water represents the source of life and natural abundance; as a force that cannot ultimately be contained, it also represents spiritual energy. So the spear was steeped in water long enough to charge it with the powers of the spirits. And once it was potent with that energy he took the spear to Namizzi and began a relocation ceremony. Rain began to fall and continued until the ceremony ended. Animals and birds were sacrificed as blood offerings, fires were burnt and the villagers feasted, sang and danced. The spirits were happy to move to the new site as the beating rains had cleansed the area. This means that the construction project will be able to go ahead without fear of angering the deities. The Busoga people have been happy to embrace change, seeing it as a positive move towards cultural progression, but they have made the changes with due respect for their spiritual welfare.

left A girl walks to the Bujagali Falls to fetch water. This is the traditional home of the spirit of Bujabald, the tutelary power which has supernatural energies crucial to the health and wellbeing of the Busoga people. It has been the site of practical and cultural changes recently.

Sedlec Ossuary
Kutná Hora, Czech Republic

Sedlec Ossuary is a small chapel beneath the Church of All Saints and close to the Cathedral Church of the Assumption of Our Lady and Saint John the Baptist. It was built during the fifteenth century in response to a chain of events leading back to 1278. During that year, Abbot Heidenreich of the Cistercian monastery in Sedlec was sent on a mission to the Holy Land by King Otakar II of Bohemia. We know that he visited Golgotha on his journey, and it is most likely that he walked there from Jerusalem, following in the footsteps of Jesus in an act of pilgrimage. When Jesus took his journey to Golgotha, the Place of the Skull, he left Jerusalem carrying the cross on which he was to be crucified. This was his great act of self-sacrifice for the forgiveness of the sins of others and it is commemorated in religious services, and also in a host of art forms, known as the Stations of the Cross or the Way of the Cross.

On arriving at Golgotha, Heidenreich fell to his knees and scooped up a handful of earth, the sacred ground from which Christ gave up his soul to God. He took the soil back to the monastery and when he sprinkled it in the cemetery he sanctified the earth in which his brethren were buried by linking it with the place of Christ's death. It was both a modest act and a momentous one – Holy Land soil strewn like sacred seed in a humble monastery. While other pilgrims claimed to have returned from the Holy Land with, say, a splinter of the True Cross; Heidenreich actually brought the Holy Land. Once this news spread everyone wanted to be buried here, with the notion that if one's earthly remains could rest in such sacred soil then safe passage to heaven must surely follow.

So the dead were sent from far and wide to this holy ground. When plague struck during the fourteenth century the burial ground was extended to accommodate the estimated 30,000 victims. Then, during the fifteenth century, a chapel was built in the cemetery, with a crypt to accommodate the thousands of bones. It is said that the task of arranging them was given to a half-blind monk who stacked them up in pyramidal form. However, during the late nineteenth century a wood carver named František Rint set about making the arrangement we see today, from approximately 40,000 skeletons. His imagination ran to a chandelier, bells, a coat of arms, patterns and swags. Yet what can today's travellers expect to experience here, beyond the spectacle of this extraordinary display? The genres of art forms known as memento mori and *vanitas* have been used since ancient times to remind us, through creative expression, of our own mortality and the brevity of mortal life. They stir inner reflections as to the nature of our existence and spur spiritual examination. And this is what is evoked so viscerally by these fantastic sculptures. While it may be chilling to stand among this display, it is also moving to contemplate the link between Heidenreich's journey and that of Christ to Golgotha, the Place of the Skull.

above A putto sits atop a display of skulls. These heavenly beings, not to be confused with cherubs, are associated with peace and prosperity, and amusingly here, with leisure and mirth. As such they bring a little lightness into the ossuary. Clearly this was the intention in the display as a whole, and while we hope that those whose remains rest here are at peace, it would be good to think that they also enjoy merriment!

right The inventive imagination of František Rint was given free rein when he embarked on this project. The woodcarver certainly had an eye for pattern and grandiose design. The chandelier, which contains all the bones of the human body, and the swags around it are a masterpiece of construction.

above and right From the lines of the crypt look unseeing eyes, as skulls and crossbones cling to the curves and balance on display stands. By placing the skull and leg bones together, the whole of the body is represented and therefore, symbolically, the soul is intact. The skull and crossbones symbol was first used by the Knights Templar, but early pirates appropriated it for their flag to lure other ships within range. In art the skull bears the symbolism of the vessel of the spirit and was therefore used by alchemists as a container in transformation processes. In Christian art it is often found at the base of crucifixion scenes, where it symbolizes mortality and Adam, who was reputedly buried at Golgotha, where he represents all of mankind.

above The display of bones takes on a life of its own, making us aware of the beauty and efficiency of the human skeleton as we go beyond qualms and trepidation to see the work of our creator.

left The charnel house in the cemetery stands above the bone-filled crypt. The bulding, its crypt and contents have found their way into a considerable number of films and works of literature, by way of artistic inspiration. As a whole, the establishment works as one big memento mori. Above ground, the tombs and graves protect their secrets.

above Rint signed his installations by writing his own name in bones elsewhere in the crypt, but not before he honoured the 40,000 or so skeletons of the deceased with their place in the unique and well-considered displays. Here the Schwarzenberg coat of arms honours the Frankish and Bohemian aristocrats who bore that name.

Le Morne Brabant
Mauritius, Indian Ocean

It has been said that Mauritius was the blueprint for heaven. Surrounded by sparkling turquoise waters in the Indian Ocean with its coral reefs, lagoons, sandy beaches and lush vegetation, the island is often cited as being an ideal holiday retreat, a haven for the weary seeking to escape the daily grind. It also offers sanctuary to several rare plants and was the only known home of the now-extinct dodo. But a small part of the island evolved as a human refuge, wrought through dire circumstance.

Slavery came to Mauritius under Dutch rule and was a stopping point for slave traders on their ungodly journeys. Throughout the island, the enslaved were exploited in the production of commodities as diverse as sugar and gunpowder, and forced to work in inhumane conditions. However, in the southwestern corner a hiding place was established, a sanctuary for runaway slaves from across the continents. Here, a peninsula called Le Morne Brabant juts into the ocean topped by a 556-metre (1,824-feet) high slab of granite and basalt rock. Pitted with caves and circled by forest and water, it offered a secluded

vantage point and dwelling place, throughout the eighteenth and early nineteenth centuries. For those escaping slavery in southeast Asia, India and the African continent, the approach would have been fraught with danger, fear and hardship. Arrival at this safe haven must have brought unbelievable relief, though life here could not have been easy. However, over time the landmark became recognized as a potent symbol of the slaves' endurance and suffering and of the injustice meted out by the free to the would-be free, the powerful to the powerless.

The bitter-sweet aspect of life for the refugee slaves is dreadfully illustrated by a misunderstanding during 1835: the residents of the rock saw a party of police approaching the hiding place, thought the worst and jumped to their deaths from the cliff rather than face punishment and renewed slavery. What they could never have imagined is that the police were in fact bringing news of freedom – that day, February 1, is celebrated by the islanders as the Annual Commemoration of the Abolition of Slavery. Because of the intensity

of experience and hardship endured by an oppressed group of people from many lands, this place has been infused with cross-cultural significance and spiritual status. Mauritius is now a multifaith island; worship and ritual reflect that fact. Another example of the triumph over slavery is a joyful annual pilgrimage to heap flowers upon the shrine of Père Laval (1803–64) in Sainte Croix. The priest arrived in Mauritius during 1841 and devoted the rest of his life to the spiritual welfare of the newly freed slaves. Out of the darkness of slavery he showed them the light of Christianity and is held in such affection that he is now remembered as the 'apostle of the black people'. These commemorative occasions are a time to celebrate the abolition of slavery and to give thanks for the value of freedom.

above left and right This landmark serves as an icon to freedom from slavery. It seems right that such symbolism should rest in the sparkling waters of the Indian Ocean, as if to symbolize that shadowy period of human history being swept away by the beauty of freedom. Although the area is now largely a holiday location, its past is recognized and treated with respect.

Panagia Evangelistria Church
Tinos, Greece

The island of Tinos sits in the Aegean Sea amid its cycladic neighbours. Some say that Aeolus, the ancient god of the winds, lived here, and certainly there are many windmills on the island, signalling the gales. Tinos was once called Ophioussa, a confluence of the Greek names for snake and water. Many of the villages still enjoy the splash of freshwater fountains but most of the snakes are gone; according to fable, they were driven out by Poseidon. A fertility god, Poseidon animated the freshets that quenched the earth and brought fecundity. He was worshipped on the island from the fourth century BC and the temple dedicated to him was extended during the third century BC to include worship of the sea nymph Amfitriti, with whom he had three offspring.

Allegiance to the old gods passed away and although it is not known when Christianity arrived on Tinos, tradition says there was a Christian monastery here by the eighth century AD and by the eleventh century a convent, Kechrovouniou, had certainly been established. This followed a dream shared by three sisters, foretelling its inception. It was here during 1822 that a nun called Pelagia had repeated dreams in which the Virgin Mary urged her to instruct the villagers to seek a sacred icon in a fallow field. At first Pelagia dismissed the dreams as imagination, but eventually she took her concerns to the bishop, who knew that another villager had had the same experience. And so the search began. After six months a figure was unearthed, a carving of the Virgin Mary kneeling in prayer. This, said to be the work of Saint Luke, the patron saint of artists, physicians and surgeons, was named Panagia Evangelistria, Our Lady of Good Tidings. And the good tidings spread, along with the blessings of Saint Luke, as the icon was found to have miraculous healing powers. Such was the significance of the figure that a church was built to house it and there it stays, having become known as the most holy icon in Greece.

Three festivals are marked in the calendar: in January, the anniversary of the discovery of the figure; in March, the Feast of the Annunciation; and in July, the anniversary of Pelagia's vision. It is said that on these occasions the healing power of the icon is especially potent. Pilgrims make their way to the island by ferry from Athens and many approach the church on their hands and knees in penance, which takes more than an hour. Repenting their

left Steps lead through the gateway and up to Our Lady of Tinos, the church of Panagia Evangelistria. This pilgrim, like so many others, will approach on her knees in an act of penance. The way is smoothed in places by carpet laid over the bumpy cobbles.

above The church, built from local marble in 1824, was made especially to house the miraculous icon. This is illuminated by hundreds of gilded lamps burning beeswax flames. Votive offerings may be in the form of symbolic objects – a baby's bib for fertility or a bandage for an injury.

sins in this act of contrition prepares them spiritually to ask for help from the Virgin. Many miracles of healing are said to have occurred here and those who are too sick to come may send a relative to act on their behalf. Votive offerings are left as symbols of thanksgiving or intercession, a tradition with its roots in ancient times when bandages and crutches were cast aside by restored patients. Healed or simply uplifted, the pilgrims leave feeling that they are walking on air.

right The main annual pilgrimage is on August 15. This day also marks the sinking of the Greek cruiser *Elli* by an Italian submarine in 1940. Pilgrims come to church to commemorate those lost and pray for continued peace, alongside those who seek to approach the icon.

below Many pilgrims who have arrived by boat make the 800 metre (2,625 feet) journey to the church from the ferry entirely on their hands and knees. To the faithful, this is all part of the pilgrimage.

ALONG THE WAY

Passing through a landscape may be an experience of beauty or poignancy, delight or displeasure, depending on all manner of variables, and many aspects of life are condensed into the acts of planning, transacting and completing the journey. Engaging with new places and people offers us a chance to understand the world a little more, and the part we play in it. This experience can be enhanced by being open to what happens along the way, listening to God and those we meet, and by being mindful. Most landscapes we pass through have been formed and furrowed by humankind, but they are also swept and washed by natural forces, elements far beyond our control. It is this human and divine relationship that we need to balance within ourselves.

left On approaching the Ise shrines in the Mie Prefecture of Japan, the pilgrim meets the simple architecture based upon ancient storehouses. Made from unvarnished cyprus wood, the buildings are thatched and topped with gold, representing divine brilliance.

Choice of transport is in many ways dependent upon the amount of time a pilgrim can give to a project, and upon ability too. But for many, walking is the preferred option. The rhythm set up by the repetitive motion of one foot in front of the other is conducive to thought and conversation. Indeed, many people walk with the intention of clearing their heads and removing themselves from the demands of work, family or chores. Walking with companions offers an opportunity for engagement that is free from the usual social mores, such as hospitality, domestic interruption and how to behave in someone else's space, so informality slips in and new rules evolve.

Inevitably within a walking pilgrimage, people fall in with others moving at a similar pace and this brings fresh contacts, enlarging the spectrum of exchange until something happens to break the pattern, and another group is formed. But the dynamics of walking with others are subtle and people assume roles. Those who move slowly will not be left behind, because someone will wait for them, while those who stride ahead may miss something valuable, but will clear obstacles and confirm

the route for those who follow. Eye contact is reduced, allowing a kind of semi-anonymity. This, and the common path, lead into depths of conversation not normally touched upon with new-found companions. Aching limbs, twists and blisters elicit sympathy and help, and everyone shares the same weather and terrain under the same sky, so this is a shared experience on many levels.

The early pilgrim walker would have taken a flask for water, shoes (or not, depending on the culture), a cloak and staff. Groups of travellers may have shared a beast of burden; camels could carry plenty, and exceed 32 kilometers (20 miles) a day without food or water, and mules and donkeys coped well with difficult terrain, but thought they knew best about the need for progress. Horses were expensive and often reserved for military purposes, and dangers beset the party in the shape of wild beasts, foul weather, extremes of temperature and the risk of injury. Seafaring posed similar challenges along with extra navigational demands. Yet despite all the difficulties, sacred journeys have always

been made. Clearly there is some reward to be found or need to be met by taking these risks and abandoning routine. For nomadic peoples and for wandering monks, travel was and is a way of life, the sacred and the mundane run in synchrony. Nowadays, pilgrims enjoy following in others' footsteps and, in some cases, feel their presence. That link with pilgrims past adds another layer of meaning and validation to an already significant process, a compound interest of spiritual value.

The Armenian Christians who gather around the Qareh Kalisa in Iran come from within that country and way beyond. Because of their faith being, at best, tolerated in this land, their journey is imbued with a different type of solidarity. There is a need to tighten cultural ties within a short space of time at the once-a-year gathering, and joy is increased because of the relaxation of the norms usually enforced in this Islamic nation. Sustenance along the way is crucial if the disorientating effects of extreme temperature, hunger and dehydration are not to tip the pilgrim into danger.

In Mexico, the Huichol use wild legumes and fruits as they move along their pilgrimage route, telling stories and seeking insights into the nature of reality through the sustenance of peyote. Elsewhere, travellers' needs are anticipated by others. The steep climb up Sri Pada is dotted with stations for rest and refreshment, and spirits are kept up by song and words of compassion. The Saint Birinus pilgrimage in Dorchester offers food and drink along its 19-kilometre (12-mile) stretch, followed by a meal after the act of worship, where an ancient painting of Saint Christopher greets and protects travellers at the destination. The form of companionship, provision and welcome vary with clime and culture, but the sentiments are universal.

below left to right Pakou Caves, Luang Prabang, Laos; the Cistercian Way, Wales, UK; Naiku and Geku Shrines, Ise, Japan; the Tombs of the Patriarchs, Hebron, West Bank.

Huichol Route
Nayarit to Huiricuta, Mexico

A Mexican pilgrimage route stretching over 800 kilometres (500 miles) from coastal Nayarit to Huiricuta is the cultural and spiritual conduit through which the indigenous Huichol people nurture their ancestral heritage and keep their religious beliefs vibrant. Along the route ancestral spirits and deities reside in the natural features of the landscape. And to the Huichol, their relationship with the spirit world is mutually sustaining and dependent. The people nourish and entertain the deities and spirits with music and dance and in turn receive harvests, health and protection. Pilgrims learn from the elders how to locate and commune with the powerful energies inherent in the sacred landscape and how to use the wisdom passed on and kept alive through practice and oral tradition.

This is a pilgrimage route where the landscape is the temple and the spiritual journey is as active an engagement as the celebration on arrival. Throughout the year people may make frequent visits to sacred points along the way, but the annual full-length pilgrimage is critical in maintaining cohesion and spiritual renewal. Distance and passage are intrinsic, for the spirits whisper their wisdom from springs, pools, rocks and wind, each message contributing its own vital share of the whole; what is heard may be punitive or encouraging, but is always imbued with ancestral authority. Chanting, oral history and performance are the shaman's means of educating the young and embedding cultural tradition, while ensuring healing and nature's abundance; this is a culture with no written heritage.

The Huichol are fully aware of the value of the elements that hold their knowledge – the deer, eagle and wolf, along with the endemic flora found in this biologically and topographically diverse landscape. These are held with a reverence that may seem arcane to outsiders, just as the outsiders' scientific or romantic appreciation may be seen to miss the point by anyone who fully engages with the spiritual whole. However, outside agencies are helping the Huichol to preserve rights of access. For example, sections of the route fenced in for cattle are to have unlockable gates in strategic places.

Some believe that the Huichol people originally came from Huiricuta and that the pilgrimage is a symbolic return to their roots, where they celebrate their heritage in visions sparked by the sacred cactus peyote in a traditional ceremony dating back though countless years.

right This *mara'akame* (shaman who leads the pilgrimage) and his family have come to a cave to pray for rain. Huichol people see care of the landscape as one of their sacred duties and frequent contact with the gods is an essential part of that responsibility.

below left and right Here at a pilgrim encampment in the state of Zacatecas, a Huichol woman takes time to sew. This young boy learns to blow the cow horn, part of the training for one who wishes to become a *mara'akame*.

Sri Pada Pilgrimage
Ratnapura, Sri Lanka

Few places on earth can claim as broad a tract of illustrious footprints as the holy mountain of Sri Pada (Adam's Peak): the Buddha, Adam, Shiva and Saint Thomas are among the holy ones who came here. Alexander the Great, Marco Polo and a host of famous poets, priests and pilgrims have climbed its steep sides, too. The nature of the mountain's physical profile has always marked it out as special from a distance, clothed as it is in exuberant forests of orchids, rhododendrons and running waters. No wonder this was thought to be the Garden of Eden!

The interfaith heritage and hospitality found at this site have a long tradition for pilgrims. The fourteenth-century papal legate Giovanni dei Marignolli took many a sacred journey, and after a prolonged spell travelling throughout the Far East he set off home via Baghdad, Damascus and Jerusalem. Troubled on his way by a storm, he sought shelter in Sri Lanka, where he met with further misfortune. However, he found his way to Sri Pada, where Buddhist monks welcomed him with brotherly hospitality and friendship. And though they were of a different faith, the traveller recognized holiness in the life, work and ministry so freely offered.

Today, the mountain receives people from Buddhist, Hindu, Christian and Islamic traditions, and facilities have had to be expanded to meet the needs of growing numbers. But despite the hospitality, this journey is not for the faint-hearted; the route to the top is arduous and reaches 2,243 metres (7,359 feet). Before beginning the ascent it is traditional to bathe in the icy stream called Seetha Gangula, then to pray for blessings and a safe passage. The gradient quickly steepens beyond the stream, but is cut in steps, and rest points offer refreshment and seats for those who wish to pace themselves. On arrival at the *indikatu pana*, or 'place of the needle', it is customary to stitch a thread into the foliage and allow the yarn to gently unravel itself alongside the path; the emptying bobbin symbolizes the loosening of worldly attachments and the thread that stretches ahead is analogous to the doctrine that guides us. This marks the time when the Buddha stopped to mend a rip in his robe; now a tangle of strands describes the gradient. Pilgrims never ask how far it is to the top, but sing and exchange the word *karunava*, which means 'compassion to you'. On arrival at the peak the traveller strikes a bell, once for each visit paid here, but not the novice whose pilgrimage is only halfway through – it is not considered complete until the traveller has returned home. The ringing of the bell is accompanied by prayers, chants and the smell of incense as pilgrims queue to honour the indentation enshrined here – the footprint of Shiva, Buddha, Adam or Saint Luke – another treasure held for all eternity.

left Sri Pada, also known as Adam's Peak, rises out of the jungle to form an iconic landmark, once used to guide seafaring vessels. It is densely scented with spice trees, speckled with gem mines, and in this photograph swirled with morning mist. Many faith groups have sacred mythology attached to the place and come to honour its significance in their thousands.

below There are 5,200 steps leading the pilgrims to the top of the mountain. They are rewarded with a stunning view, the exhilaration of visiting the shrine and the satisfaction of striking the bell at the top – if they have been before! The descent completes the pilgrimage.

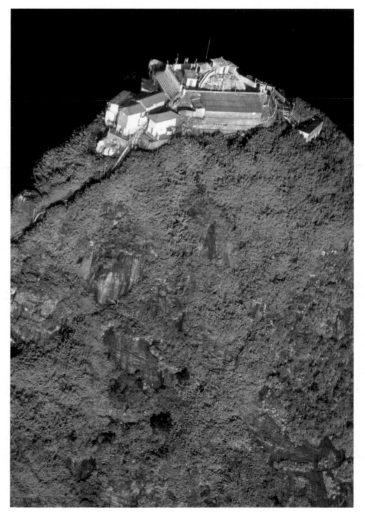

above These pilgrims are waiting to greet the morning sun and jostle for space to witness the phenomenon that daybreak brings. Being here for this spectacular event is one of the pilgrims' ambitions and involves climbing by night, which takes several hours.

above The shadow of the summit of Sri Pada is cast in a great triangle across the valley to the west. The pilgrim has the choice of starting from the village of Maskeliya, on the eastern slopes, or from Ratnapura, to the southwest of the peak. Many travellers climb through the night in order to watch the spectacular sunrise from the summit.

above A weary pilgrim reaches the top of the mountain, having no doubt called at the shrine at the base for a period of quiet contemplation before embarking upon the climb. There is a season for pilgrimage here, dictated by the weather. For safety, December to May is the time to come, with the full moon announcing the season's start and finish.

Naiku and Geku Shrines
Ise, Japan

Ise Jingu is a complex of over 100 shrines, familiarly known as O-Ise-San and recognized as the spiritual home of the Shinto religion. The two most significant points within it are the Naiku and Geku shrines, dedicated to Amaterasu Omikami, the sun goddess, and Toyouke Omikami, the goddess of grain, respectively. According to legend, the Naiku shrine was established following a 20-year sacred journey. Emperor Suinin sent his daughter, Yamatohime-no-mikoto, to find a suitable and permanent place at which to worship Amaterasu Omikami, the Shinto deity. Since time immemorial she had been worshipped at the Imperial Palace and was an ancestor of the Imperial family. So Yamatohime-no-mikoto set off on an epic trail that took her through the old provinces of Omi and Mino. But on arrival at Ise, the voice of Amaterasu Omikami announced that she would like to live forever in this blessed, glorious place of sea and mountains; Yamatohime-no-mikoto's journey had ended.

So the Naiku shrine was built to house and worship the goddess, embodied in the sacred mirror that holds her image. Because of its bright clarity the mirror also symbolizes honesty, wisdom and the sun. At the Geku shrine there is a twice-daily ceremony honouring Toyouke Omikami, who served food to Amaterasu Omikami. These shrines are set in different parts of the city but are linked by a choice of two pilgrim routes, and it is customary to visit Geku first and then move on to Naiku, perhaps calling at some of the lesser sanctuaries along the way. On arrival at the shrines, pilgrims wash their mouths and hands, then, before worship, perform two very deep bows and clap twice at chest height. The hands are held together in prayer, which is finished with one final deep bow. These simple acts demonstrate respect, focus and gratitude.

As at other sacred sites, there is a cycle of ceremonies and festivals here, the greatest and most unusual being the Shikinen Sengu ceremony, which has been celebrated every two decades since AD 690. It entails the exact replication and replacement of the entire shrine, on a site of identical proportions; followed by the renewal of all ceremonial objects and the symbolic transfer of the *kami* (natural forces or powers) to the new shrine. Thus the spiritual energies are refreshed and invigorated. A project on this huge scale demands a tremendous amount of cedar wood, which must have reached a

left Shinto rites are full of symbolism. This priest, seen in solitary prayer, will have undertaken a period of abstinence in preparation for greeting pilgrims, in order to purify himself. At the beginning of any ceremony, he will rinse his hands, mouth, and hands again to symbolically cleanse his whole body.

certain age to offer the required girth and height. Because of the Shinto respect for nature, sustainable forests have been ceremonially planted and cared for, as the forest itself is a shrine. Nothing is undertaken hurriedly or even with the convenience of modern technology. Felling the trees demands the permission of the forest deities and the return of the top of the tree to the roots, thus only the middle is taken. The practice of using a thoughtful, ritualistic approach ensures the continuity of tradition. Moreover, it passes ancient ways into the future and keeps the Shinto faith alive; this is the Way of the Kami – and the meaning of Shinto.

right Every 20 years the shrines are reconstructed to renew their sacred energies. This demands a huge number of appropriate timbers. In a system called Shikinen Sengu, which has been observed for 1,300 years, each spring the supreme priest and other priests bless the planting of about 500 Japanese cyprus trees. These will, in due course, be ceremonially felled and used in temple-building. All who take part in the ceremonies must wear traditional uniforms and chant appropriate words. The deities are asked to grant permission to cut the trees, and to protect all involved, especially the carpenters. Wood is transported by river in a ceremony called Okihiki-gyoji, or 'pulling of the wood'.

above This is the Way of Moss on the pilgrim route to the shrines. The Shinto faith has a high regard for nature; the *kami* (Shinto deities) are present in all nature's manifestations, such as the moss along this wooded path and the power of the full moon. Nature is honoured in ceremonies such as Kangetsukai, which is the ceremony for observing the full moon.

above The Naiku and Geku shrines are linked by pilgrim routes which are dotted with lesser shrines along the way. Many pilgrims stop off at these shrines in preparation for the ceremonies. *Komainu* (canine statues), located outside the shrines, act as guardians. The hound on the right has its mouth open as if chanting 'ah', while the one opposite hums 'um': together these are the sacred syllables of the universe, 'aum' or 'om'.

Pak Ou Caves
Luang Prabang, Laos

The culture of Laos is largely influenced by the Theravada school of Buddhism, with less than 40 per cent of the population adhering purely to the spirit worship which was practised here before Buddhism arrived. However, the two systems are not mutually exclusive and there is a degree of syncretism. This can be seen in the small city of Luang Prabang, which plays a proud part in the culture's ancient creation myth and is also home to around 40 Buddhist temples. The fusion of faith and culture is narrated through temple architecture, the visual arts and ritual; at times the air vibrates with the resonance of prayer bells ringing awareness of the sacred out of the shrines, into the streets and onto the banks of the Mekong River. Running for more than 4,000 kilometres (2,485 miles), the Mekong visits six countries and when it reaches landlocked Laos, its basin encompasses 90 per cent of the

left This display of buddha statuary is in the lower cave at Pak Ou. People have been worshipping in these caves for some 2,000 years; before Buddhism, the river spirits were the objects of devotion. However, once Buddhism arrived in Laos, the old faith was either replaced or adapted to the new.

below Monks descend from the upper cave, Tham Phum, to the lower cavern, which is called Tham Ting. Monks are the main practitioners of faith in Laos, with many young men entering a monastery in preparation for maturity and marriage. This is also a crucial opportunity for boys from poor families to be educated, and they may choose to extend their stay.

country. Not only does it offer transport, food and water, it also houses the water spirits that help with fishing and protect the boats.

Pilgrims leave Luang Prabang and take the 25-kilometre (15½-mile) boat ride for approximately two hours through stunning scenery to the confluence with the Nam Ou – 'the Rice Bowl River'. Close to this spot are the Pak Ou Caves, cut high above the waters in the sandstone cliffs. Once the home of Buddhist monks, they now serve as shrines for pilgrims wishing to pay homage to the spirits of the caves and to the crowds of Buddha statues that fill these sacred spaces. On arrival, a 10-metre (33-foot) flight of steps leads from the landing stage to Tham Ting, the lower of the two caves, which is entered through a huge and jagged mouth, gaping wide above the river. Here, buddhas of all shapes and sizes wait to greet pilgrim and tourist alike. Daylight shows them to be made from stone, horn, resin or wood and they are plain, painted or gilded. The buddhas jostle for space on shelves and ledges, and crowd across the floor. Incense fills the air along with the hum of chanting and the whisper of prayer. As the pilgrim turns to leave, some sculptures fall into silhouette against the light, the darkened forms framed by the mouth of the cave. Another flight of steps leads to the upper cave, known as Tham Phum. No sunlight reaches this space, where candles flicker and smoke. Torches pick out details on yet more statues, and throw shadows across the figures and onto the walls. Faces light up, surfaces glimmer and glint. The language of the Buddha is signed in gesture, pose and attribute; for although the craftwork

appears decorative, its primary purpose is to express a message – the hands can signify preaching, meditation, wish granting and more. In the darkness, a torch beam may settle on one sign to the exclusion of others, bringing thoughts into focus. In excluding daylight, the depth of the cave demands a light source. And where the tourist sees surface, the pilgrim finds symbolism.

above left The faithful kneel to make oblations at statues in the mouth of the lower cave. The position of the caves above the river seems to put this sacred space into another realm. It is both natural and manmade, secret and open, creating a unique atmosphere of calm and splendour.

above right About 4,000 statues have accumulated in the caves over a long period of time. Votive candles, flowers and incense are some of the offerings left by pilgrims. The *mudras*, symbolic hand gestures shown by the sculptures, tell of preaching, teaching and more.

right Arrival by river is the safest way to access the caves. This image shows how craftspeople have adapted the mouth of the cave into a dignified approach which also shows respect for its natural forms. The jagged rocks above act as tutelary forms, as if guarding the sacred interior.

Saint Birinus Pilgrimage
Oxfordshire, England

The beautiful historic Abbey Church of Saint Peter and Saint Paul, Dorchester-on-Thames, now acts as parish church to a vibrant congregation, who abbreviate the name to Dorchester Abbey. This is also the destination of those who come to honour Saint Birinus at the end of an annual summer pilgrimage.

On setting sail for England, the Italian Bishop Birinus found that he needed to return for his Eucharistic cloth, left ashore in Genoa. So he boldly stepped overboard and walked to shore through the stormy waters, collected the cloth, then retraced his steps back to the boat, which had waited as if rooted in the water. The astonishment of all aboard increased when they noted that the bishop's garments remained dry. Clearly, this was no ordinary man! The travellers became his first converts. It was probably the wise counsel of Pope Honorius I (AD 625–638) that spurred Birinus' mission to England's shores during AD 634. Aiming to 'sow the seeds of our holy faith in the most inland and remote regions of the English', he found the people of the Thames Valley so shamefully heathen as to stop him in his tracks. He would minister here among the West Saxons. The pagan King Cynegils tolerated Birinus' preaching, allowing him to use the landmark Churn Knob (in Blewbury, Berkshire) for his first sermon. It was not until some time later, though, that Cynegils converted and was baptized by Birinus on the banks of the river at Doric, now called Dorchester-on-Thames. Performing baptism is a joy for any priest, but this conversion had the distinction of bringing Christianity into a hitherto pagan royal household; Cynegil's family also bowed their heads for the waters of baptism and Christianity began to flow here from that time onwards. The King gave Dorcic to Birinus as his see, and the Abbey Church that stands today marks the site of his Saxon cathedral.

On Birinus' death during AD 649, his shrine became a place of pilgrimage, and although his remains were later removed to Winchester, an annual pilgrimage to the shrine continues. This 19-kilometre (12-mile) walk begins at Churn Knob and makes its way through fields and villages, pausing at stations along the way. Crosses bearing prayers call the walkers to moments of quiet supplication, before companionship and destination call, and so the party moves on. The path also traces pre-Christian sacred sites: a wellspring at the village of Brightwell was dedicated to Bertha, the Saxon goddess of moon and springs, while Castle Hill, once an iron age hill fort near Little Wittenham, is still a place for seasonal votive offerings. The approach to Dorchester passes close to the confluence of the rivers Thames and Thame, an early auspicious point for sending prayers to the rising sun. This being England, tea and cakes are never far away and along the pilgrimage route they are the hospitality freely offered at Brightwell and at Saint Birinus Roman Catholic Church, the last station before the shrine. For this pilgrimage is truly ecumenical, calling up to 800 Anglicans, Catholics, Orthodox and other Christian traditions not only to walk together but to share in worship around Birinus' shrine. The styles of music, prayer and sermon reflect that spectrum; Gregorian chant may give way to the vigour of a brass band, loud alleluias to prayer from a single voice. The single voice of Birinus preached seeds of faith, which flower still.

left The stained-glass window in the abbey shows Birinus baptising King Cynegils, which happened on the banks of the River Thame, a little upstream from its confluence with the Thames and close to where the abbey now stands. Birinus is shown with the mitre and crosier, denoting his status as a bishop.

right On the north side of the abbey is the Cloister Garden, which as the name suggests was once the site of the monastic cloisters. Today this garden is perfect for quiet reflection, with the cross as a focal point. However, the garden is also used for feasting and celebration at the end of the annual Saint Birinus Pilgrimage.

The Passion Plays
Oberammergau, Germany

Oberammergau is nestled in the beautiful landscape of the Ammergau Alps, and what draws the pilgrim here is a journey with two distinct aspects. It is a temporal cycle of 10 years for the residents and a pilgrimage for those who choose to visit a unique event here. But it is so much more as well. It was in 1633, and halfway through Europe's Thirty Years' War, that this Bavarian village took the decision to insulate itself from the outside world in an attempt to avoid the Black Death that was sweeping the continent. But a young man who sought safe haven sneaked inside and with him came the plague. Almost half the population died in a short space of time. The authorities turned to God and vowed that if he would spare the rest of the villagers, they would

enact a drama, a mystery play expressing the life and self-sacrifice of Christ during the week before Christ's execution. This would affirm the community's faith in God while shouting belief and praise and inspiring those who watched. Moreover, the people promised to repeat the play for the rest of their days. Miraculously, no more lives were lost to the plague here. God had answered their prayers, now the villagers must fulfil their promise.

So, in 1634, the first play was performed, in the Black Death cemetery, and has continued to be presented every 10 years. The performers, musicians, stagehands and technicians, about 2,000 in all, come from the community. Their dedication even extends to a 'hair

decree day', when men must begin growing their hair and beards for the next production! Preparation for the huge event takes tremendous team effort, commitment and skill, but the whole project is born out of gratitude and the conviction that art can change lives. The intention is to explore the mystery and depth of a relationship with God; for those who take part this is a journey of devotion sustained by teamwork and the weight of history. The audience see the journey as a pilgrimage taken in preparation for a dramatic event and many call at other sacred places along the way; these other stations establish spiritual receptivity in order to experience the aesthetic rush of music, acting, colour and crowd, all expressed in the landscape which sparked the idea. But

previous page Oberammergau in Bavaria, Germany, is famous for its Passion Play, which has been a part of the town's sacred culture since 1634. It is also known for its tradition of woodcarving and Lüftlmalerei, the frescos which show religious or cultural narratives. We can see a fine example of both crafts at this shop of sacred carvings.

left Kloster Ettal Monastery, near Oberammergau, adds to the pilgrim attraction of the area. It first flourished as a pilgrim destination in the early eighteenth century. Pilgrimage to this remote site would originally have been difficult. It is situated in an alpine pass and, although isolation was not a problem for the self-sufficient monks, it did pose an extra challenge for pilgrims.

here, performance is worship. No applause cuts the air, and no photographs are taken; the audience and actors are sharing in a reverent act of devotion. Groups of people book their tickets years in advance in the knowledge that attendance will be a life- and faith-affirming experience. The six-hour performance is given to a crowd of over 5,000, all keenly aware of their situation being analogous to the crowd in Jerusalem who watched Jesus all those years ago. Actor and audience take part to illuminate more brightly their understanding of the Christian message. Giving and receiving are mutually dependent and here each side grows and learns from sharing this unique experience, where the total is worth even more than the sum of the parts.

right above The Passion Play has a cast that includes all age groups. Here we see children at the foot of the cross, along with the saints and angels, all against a backdrop of Christ giving his blessing. It takes years to plan and produce the plays, which involve the whole community serving as actors, technicians, carpenters and costume designers.

right below In all, about 2,000 people are involved in making the play. This tradition was started in response to the elders' prayer to God during the Thirty Years' War, beseeching him to spare the inhabitants from the bubonic plague, which stalked Europe at that time.

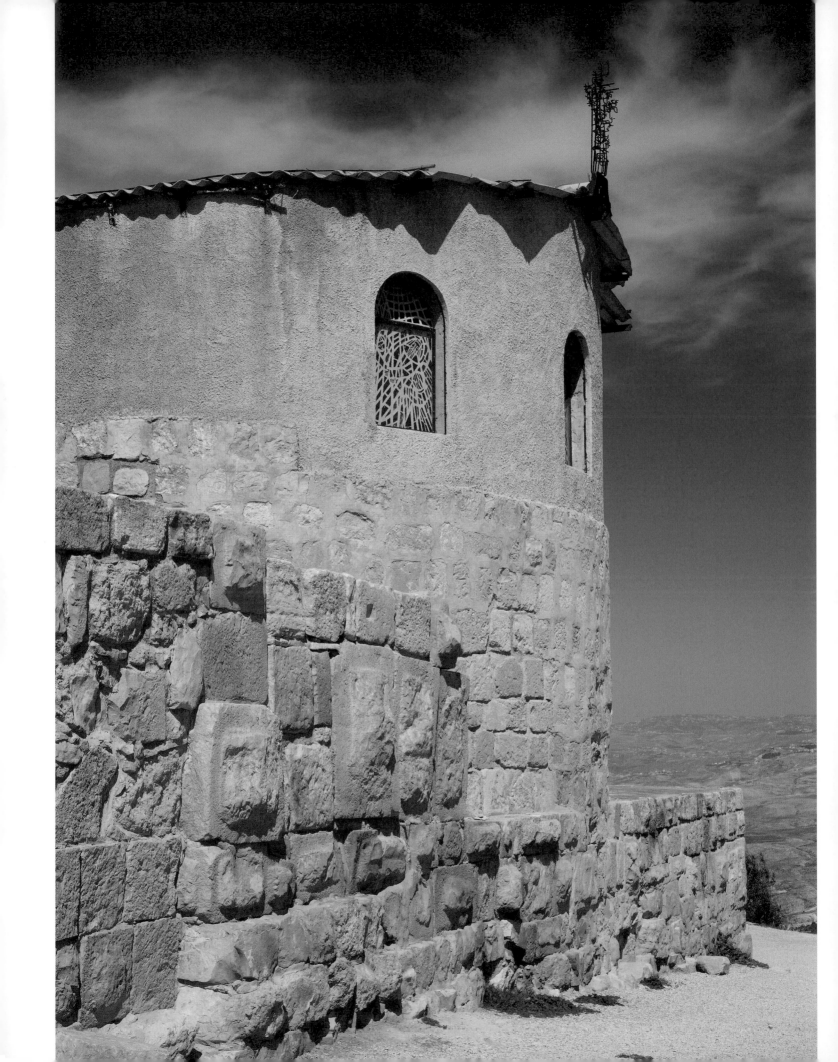

Mount Nebo
Jordan

The book of Isaiah tells us that Nebo was once worshipped as a sacred mountain, and archaeological remains confirm that it was inhabited in antiquity. From the top, the sweeping panorama visible from the mountain offers a wide and distant horizon looking across the Bible lands and invites the visitor to picture sacred history. The desert of Judah, Bethlehem, Jerusalem and the Mount of Olives are just some of the places a clear day will reveal to sharp eyes. Pope John Paul II visited here during the year 2000 while on a tour of the Holy Land, seeking to improve interfaith relations. He prayed for all the people of the Promised Land and asked God that Jews, Muslims and Christians should receive the gift of true peace, justice and fraternity. In naming those three faiths he embraced everyone who has ever been touched by the word of God as understood by those who wrote the Old Testament, and the sacred texts that followed it.

Like so many others, the Pope visited to stand on the spot where Moses was shown by God the extent of the lands promised to the people he had led for so long. We are told that although he was 120 years old, he was still strong and his vision was keen. Nevertheless,

setting eyes on the view was the closest he could get; he would never step into the Promised Land. For Moses knew he would die here, unseen by the tribes who waited below for his return. Moses' sacred journey had been a long one, starting from the moment he was found abandoned in a basket floating on the River Nile. His life was extraordinary and destined for leadership. He led the Israelites out of slavery in Egypt to survive plague and peril, sustained by the mysterious manna from heaven and water that sprang miraculously from stones.

This physical and spiritual direction continues to hold Moses as an important prophet for Jews, Christians, Muslims and Mormons, among others. And this is why to journey to Mount Nebo holds dear significance to so many people. The journey up the mountain follows the prophet's solitary footsteps, the arrival honours his life and death and the view takes in the sacred landscape that for Moses and his people represented the future. It is poignant to share the prophet's viewpoint beneath that same sun from the very spot where Moses considered all that had led him here. Today's pilgrims may

left This church at the top of Mount Nebo dates from the sixth or seventh century. It incorporates the ancient baptistry, where many began their sacred journey of life with Christ through the waters of baptism. Today the church is known for its splendid mosaics, some say the best in Jordan, though the simplicity of the architecture belies the artwork held within.

below At the top of Mount Nebo we can see the view of the Promised Land that Moses saw, and we can stand where he stood. The view extends to the Dead Sea, the Jordan Valley, to Jericho and across to the Mount of Olives. An unimaginable amount of history has been witnessed by this landscape, some of which is perhaps still to be uncovered.

travel with organized excursions or by bus and foot. The 187-metre (2,680-feet) climb will reward them with the Memorial Church of Moses, an ancient baptistry dated to AD 531 and the foundations of an early monastery. But there's more than that: many of the indoor spaces are beautifully decorated with mosaic patterns and pictures which draw the eye away from the outer landscape to the sheltered spaces, as if reminding the visitor that inner vistas are informed by looking outwards, reciprocal views which require careful balance if spiritual insight is to be gained.

above The exquisite mosaic floor of the baptistry dates to the early sixth century, and leads to the cruciform font in the floor. Four bands of figures show hunting and pastoral scenes, which are decorated with trees and flowers, all of which have been arranged with wonderful skill and detail, as has the decorative border.

above The Brazen Serpent sculpture stands at the top of the mountain. Made by Italian artist Giovanni Fantoni, it incorporates sacred symbolism from both the Old and New Testaments: the bronze serpent that Moses made in the desert to heal those who had suffered snake bites and the shape of Jesus' crucifixion. It is not unlike the Asclepius Staff, still used as a symbol of healing in pharmacies and health agencies.

above Also on the mountain stands this memorial stone to Moses, humble yet dignified in its simplicity. Established by the Franciscans at the Monastery of Siyagha, it marks the spot where Moses viewed the Promised Land: 'Go up into the Abarim Range to Mount Nebo in Moab, across from Jericho, and view Canaan, the land I am giving the Israelites as their own possession' (Deuteronomy 32: 49–52).

Ovoos
Mongolia

It was the great ruler Chingis Khan (Gengis Khan) in the thirteenth century who first identified the spiritual qualities found in Bogd Khan, Burkhan Khaldun and Otgon Tenger, three mountains in Mongolia that have been protected down the ages by virtue of their sacredness. It is thought that he followed Tengriism, the belief path traditionally trodden by the nomads of Mongolia who revere what they call the 'Eternal Blue Heaven' and live with deep respect for nature. In Tengriism the spirits of the earth, sky and ancestors provide sustenance and balance, which must be maintained through wholesome, respectful lifestyles. In keeping these high standards a person aims to strengthen his soul, the Wind Horse. It is within this inner, essential quality that a person must honour the relationship between earth and sky, from which flows spiritual health. Any imbalance brought about by disaster or transgression weakens the soul and calls for shamanic intervention to put things right again; this is for the good of both the individual and of the outside world.

Approximately half of Mongolians are nomadic, living in circular, felt-covered tents called ghers or yurts. The gher represents the universe in microcosm, its form echoing the paths of the planets, sun, moon and cardinal points. This conceives of the centre of the earth and all the three-dimensional axes being linked by a domed outline, holding the elements of this world in a cohesive mass within the cosmos while symbolizing the turning of the year and the temporal rhythms of the seasons. Within the walls of the gher, the domestic arrangements and movements of the dwellers pay homage to this concept. So, upon entering the door, which faces south, one must follow the path of the heavenly bodies: the men's saddles are kept on the western side for heavenly protection and at the north is the altar; turning east the area for food preparation is minded by the sun. The fire takes central position and, representing ancestral links, must not be desecrated with rubbish or scraps. When it is time to move on to fresh grazing, the gher is packed away and taken to new pastures, along with the animals.

Along the way, ovoos – cairns of stone or wood – mark auspicious places for worship, and alignment with the path of the sun is continued here; ovoos are circled three times sunwise, and the spirits are asked for protection on the journey. Furthermore, votive offerings may be left – for example a length of blue silk, symbolic of the Eternal

right This ovoo stands near Ulaanbaatar, which is 1,350 metres (4,429 feet) above sea level, landlocked and known as the coldest capital city in the world. The ovoo, built of stones, pays homage to the Eternal Blue Heaven, indicated by the blue cloths tied around the symbolic gate. The ovoo is circled three times, sunwise, and then more stones or silk are added.

Blue Heaven, or extra stones added to the pile. These cairns may have evolved from burial and funeral rituals and are now associated with the ancestors and with shamanic activity, because from the ovoo the shaman may soar through spirit planes to the secret realms of the upper and lower worlds, returning with wisdom and solutions. It is said that Chingis Khan spent three days in prayer at the ovoo on the top of Burkhan Khaldun, invoking guidance before embarking upon major strategies. By removing himself to the Eternal Blue Heaven in order to strengthen his soul in readiness to face the world, he clearly recognized spiritual sustenance as a source of earthly strength.

top This ovoo has been topped with symbolic objects, which are offerings relating to need or as expressions of gratitude. When ovoos are circled in a sunwise direction, the traveller is following the paths of the heavenly bodies and thus aligning him or herself with nature.

above In Mongolia, the Lunar New Year is a time to celebrate the end of winter, and the season is called White Moon Holiday or Tsagaan Sar. It is a family time which involves honouring the elders, and enjoying special food and drink. This man sacrifices a glass of vodka to the Eternal Blue Sky at the ovoo.

left A Mongolian Tsaatan hunting party makes a votive offering at this ovoo. These reindeer herdsmen, numbering only 30 to 40 families now, enjoy a culture that is unchanged since the Ice Age; their relationship to the landscape, and therefore their existence, is closely tied to the shaman's ritual.

The Tombs of the Patriarchs
Hebron, West Bank

Abraham, the Old Testament patriarch, was sent by God to Hebron and he settled here among the sacred trees of Mamre where the leafy glades would have expressed the link between heaven and earth. Deeply significant for all of the Abrahamic faiths are the Tombs of the Patriarchs, established here. The book of Genesis goes on to tell us that Abraham bought a plot of land in which to bury his wife Sarah. The field in question contained a grotto, known as the Cave of Machpelah; this became not only Sarah's burial place, but in time that of Abraham. Their sons Isaac and Jacob were later buried there too, along with their respective wives Rebekah and Leah. The shrine we see today was built to embrace the cave and holds deep spiritual and historical resonance due to the roles of those patriarchs and matriarchs in the establishment of the Abrahamic faiths.

For the Jewish people it has always been a pilgrim destination, a place to gather and pray, second in significance to only the Western Wall of the Temple in Jerusalem. King Herod was responsible for building both of these structures during the first century BC, and although the temple is long gone we can visualize its aesthetic based on the architecture here. However, its relevance has always drawn spiritual travellers and under the Byzantines and Crusaders it became a Christian church. When Hebron came under Muslim rule, Jews were not allowed to climb higher than the seventh step, approaching what was now declared a mosque.

The tombs sit along the ancient route known variably as the King's Highway, the Patriarch's Highway and the Ridge Road. This most ancient route has been in constant use since before it was travelled by Abraham himself; it linked Mesopotamia with Canaan, the conduit between many of the ancient places where much of sacred history was enacted. For instance, it was along this road that Rebekah was chosen as a bride for Isaac. Abraham instructed his oldest servant to travel to his birthplace and seek a suitable young woman, secure in the knowledge that God would send a messenger, an angel to prepare things. The servant took a caravan of camels and made his way along the King's Highway to Mesopotamia, where he stopped to take water at the well and to pray silently for guidance. This came in the form of an understanding between the man and God. What followed was the precise realization of that agreement: the girl Rebekah came to the well and offered water to

right The Tombs of the Patriarchs are sacred to Jews, Christians and Muslims because of the biblical figures buried here. This site is within the ancient city of Hebron, in the lands the Bible calls Judea. Great stone slabs used to enclose the tombs, in a structure instigated by Herod the Great, 73–4 BC.

the servant and his camels as predicted. The servant knew this to be an affirmative sign of the girl's suitability for Isaac. She agreed to meet Isaac and, with her family's consent, to set out along the highway until they met him at the Well of the Living One Who Sees Me; the two were united in marriage and now lie together in the tomb at Hebron.

Approaching this sacred place via that famous route must stir mixed feelings in the 300,000 pilgrims who visit each year. Access to the site is currently contentious and limited because of its shared significance to those who seek different routes to God.

above Muslim worshippers show their respects to the biblical figures by touching their heads to the ground in prayer. They refer to this site as the Ibrahini Mosque or Sanctuary of Abraham. Over the centuries, the structure has changed format and ownership, and is still the subject of controversy as well as being hallowed ground.

top right Each of the tombs is marked with headstones and decoration. The whole site is remarkable for its ancient archaeology and the symbolism of what it represents both religiously and politically. Jewish teaching states that this site was chosen for the tombs because it stood next to the Garden of Eden. It is also said that to worship here will bring success to those seeking a spouse.

bottom right The Cave of Machpelah is Judaism's name for the site, and here we see Jews gathering to mark the season of Sukkot, and to remember their forefathers' time in the desert. It is also an occasion when this community has access to the site and their celebrations spill out of the building and into the surrounding plaza, for special music and festivities.

The Cistercian Way
Wales

The Cistercian order was founded at Cisteaux, now known as Cîteaux, in France during 1098. The monks' practice was one of simplicity, selflessness and worldly poverty. They rejected the finery and excessive comfort of other monasteries and busied themselves with practical industry balanced by spiritual purity. The order spread throughout Europe and arrived in Wales as early as 1131, first at Tintern Abbey and then moving on to at least 15 other sites throughout the kingdom. Here, the landscape was conducive to the Cistercians' requirements: water, wood and stone were in plentiful supply and the soil was fertile and well drained. Known as the White Monks because of their dress, they had a far-reaching effect on medieval Wales; their influence reached into the local communities, as people were employed to supply services in smithies, quarries, mills and so on. Furthermore, specialist skills were imported via the Cistercians' network and so even the remotest parts of the country could benefit from outside innovations. Thus agriculture and industry grew from the monastic influx and inventiveness.

However, during the sixteenth century the dissolution of the monasteries crushed this way of life and the monastic movement was never the same again. To mark the 900th anniversary of the birth of the Cistercian movement, a group of individuals and organizations in Wales set about tracing a path between all the Cistercian abbeys in the land, both ancient and modern. This route covers more than 1,000 kilometres (620 miles) up and down the length of the country; in places it leads along original pilgrim routes; elsewhere it follows ancient earthworks such as Offa's Dyke, the mysterious ditch and rampart boundary between the ancient Kingdom of Powys and neighbouring Mercia. It also passes through mining villages, opens onto cycle tracks and noses through leafy woodlands. Thus it feels its way along the country's marks and contours where sacred and secular history reveal themselves and offer up their stories. Where necessary, new footpaths have been created, allowing travellers to tread where previously the public could not venture. The route gives pilgrims the chance to recognize and honour the effect the Cistercians had upon the Welsh landscape and to pray where they prayed. The path calls at lesser-known sacred places too: miracle sites, prehistoric caves and stone alignments. Holy wells are visited, such as the trio in the grounds of the ancient church of Saint Lawrence in Gumfreston. Here, the waters carry various minerals from their different sources; this triple manifestation

left The Cistercian Way is a pilgrim route which passes through the length and breadth of Wales, visiting all of that country's Cistercian monasteries and other sacred places along the way. Tintern Abbey, shown here, has been the inspiration of many landscape painters.

of life-giving power and healing is likely to have been venerated long before the church adopted the holy ground.

The variety of landscape and the way in which its sacredness has been articulated and venerated by people down the ages make this a pilgrimage to be taken without haste. And the watery elements for which Wales is known keep it lush; shifting cloud displays the extremes of light and shade, which sharpen the senses and keep them alert to the joy of being in glorious surroundings. Recognizing the beauty of creation can be the spark that kindles spiritual awakening.

right In its days as a working monastery, Tintern Abbey must have been a breathtaking sight and a hive of industry too. Today's pilgrims can feel the faith of its builders and former inhabitants. They may also enjoy the comforts of modern hospitality, before setting off to their next destination.

below Saint Tudno's churchyard on the Great Orme headland enjoys exhilarating views across the cliffs and the Irish Sea. The area has many freshwater springs, a welcome joy for thirsty pilgrims. One wells up in Ogof Llech, a cave said to have been used by the sixth-century monk, Tudno, who also established the church here.

Qareh Kelisa
West Azerbaijan, Iran

In the northwest of the Islamic Republic of Iran sits the Chaldoran Plateau in the province of West Azerbaijan, and therein nestles a cluster of Armenian Christian monasteries and chapels. While it may seem incongruous to find them here, their assertive presence in the landscape speaks of a confidence and determination expressed through the sturdy elegance of the architecture. One of the buildings is said to have been established on the tomb of Jesus' apostle Thaddeus, martyred for preaching Christianity, and it is to this spot that an annual pilgrimage has been making its way for the last half century.

Following Jesus' instruction to the apostles to preach the message of repentance and forgiveness throughout the world, Thaddeus travelled to Armenia, working for some of the time with Bartholomew, where the apostles' words bore fruit and many people began to follow Christ. Thus the faith became rooted in that land. Tradition tells that Thaddeus came to this spot in Iran, and established the first monastery around AD 68, supplanting a pagan temple. Iranians call this the Qareh Kelisa, or the Black Church, after the dark volcanic rock used to rebuild the edifice following an earthquake during the fourteenth century.

To the Iranian-Armenians this is the Tadeh Monastery, and one of the country's oldest Christian landmarks. While earthquakes have caused structural damage, and invasions and oppression have blighted the monastery's history, yet it housed the faith until 1948 when the last priest fell ill. In fact there is now just one service held here each year, but its significance extends way beyond the embrace of the valley. Determined that the sacredness of this distinguished site should continue to be honoured, the church authorities of Tabriz, the region's largest city, instigated a pilgrimage here during 1954 for Armenian Christians living in Islamic Iran. This has established a new tradition, and Armenian pilgrims now also come from the Lebanon, Syria and beyond. The journey demands a huge commitment and tremendous effort: the site is remote, high and difficult to access with no permanent accommodation, shops or facilities to make things easy. Yet thousands come here to live in tents, cooking on open fires and sharing in song, dance and worship. For this pilgrimage not only celebrates the Christian faith and Thaddeus' teaching, it consolidates Armenian tradition and connectedness among the diaspora. Furthermore, on this one occasion, non-Christians are not allowed here and thus there is a welcome relaxation of the day-to-day rules imposed by the Iranian authorities. Among other things this means that women may shed the chador (a loose cloak that covers the body from head to toe) and wear clothes of their own choosing. The pinnacle of the celebrations is the annual church service, an event that could be seen as one of privation and practical difficulties or as an oasis of fraternal and religious delight and freedom. Saint Thaddeus is the patron saint of lost causes and desperate situations and clearly his guardianship has not left the Tadeh. Seen from afar, the monastery sits low in the landscape; draw close and it soars above you to the sky, illustrating that what you experience depends upon your perspective.

left Armenian Christians who worship here may relax away from the usual constraints known to them in this Islamic country. Here, the women cover their heads for prayer, but once formal worship is over they may dress as they please and enjoy the religious and cultural celebrations normally frowned upon. Only Christians are allowed to come here for the pilgrimage.

right The Qareh Kelisa, or Black Church, takes its name from the black stone which was included in the construction. Armenian Christians living in Iran make their way here for the feast of the first-century missionary, Saint Thaddeus.

Lake Titicaca
Peru and Bolivia

Sacred Lake Titicaca has a wealth of mythology and an ancient history of pilgrimage relating to various interpretations of cosmology. The shoreline, waters and islands all play a part in hosting aspects of the sacred, drawing pilgrims for a variety of reasons. The enormous size of the lake feeds its mythical and mysterious status. Being 190 kilometres long (118 miles) and 80 kilometres wide (50 miles), it borders Bolivia and Peru and its waters plunge down to 284 metres (932 feet). The shoreline is more than 1,000 kilometres (620 miles) long and it is visited by those seeking fertility at numerous small shrines and by pilgrims to towns such as lakeside Copacabana, Bolivia's most sacred destination.

Here is found a syncretism between the ancient Aymara religion and the Catholic faith brought by the Spanish, a religious interweaving aided by apparent parallels between Pachamama ('Mother Earth') and the role of the mother of Christ, the Virgin Mary. Pilgrims come here to honour the miraculous sixteenth-century statue, the Dark Virgin of the Lake. It is reputed that during 1576 a fishing boat was tossed about by a dreadful storm that raged above the lake; but on praying for help, the Virgin Mary appeared and took the fishermen to safety. In gratitude, the men built a shrine in the Virgin's honour, including a statue that appeared to have captured her marvellous powers – many more miracles have been attributed to the figure and now pilgrims flock to the Basilica de la Virgen de Candelaria to see her, although the carving processed on festive occasions is a replica; the original must stay in the basilica for fear of rousing another angry storm.

The waters of the lake are sacred to the Aymara people, who journey to their Mamacota ('Mother Lake'), source of feminine healing energies, and where *yatitis*, the Aymara shamans, offer cleansing through chanting, herbs and incense. The town is linked by boat to the Isla del Sol, the sacred Island of the Sun, where it is said that the first Inca, Manco Cápac, materialized from out of the hallowed stone Titikala. As he did so, the darkness which had engulfed the world dissolved, revealing the rock to be the sun's abode. At this spot a temple was built, and later a convent for the chosen women, or *mamaconas*, along with a hostel for pilgrims. The island's counterpart, Isla de la Luna, holds intense feminine powers; it is the dwelling place of the Inca goddess Mama Quilla. Although the Incan architecture

right The waters of Lake Titicaca lap both Bolivian and Peruvian shores; these and the islands play a part in the water's sacred mythology. It is the largest lake in South America. Reed boats are the everyday mode of transport for the people who live here.

dates to 1500, some of the structures date from at least 500 BC and indicate pilgrim routes, stations and offerings from that early time. Thus the Inca recognized the earlier sanctity here and made it their own. On yet another island, Amantani, are two temple-topped mountains, one dedicated to Pachamama and one to Pachatata, ('Father Earth'). On January 18 each year their sanctity is honoured by a pilgrimage at which the local people don their traditional costumes and climb up to the temples in the realm of the sky. On descending, they make ritual offerings of coca leaves, grains and liquor to the benevolent earth.

left Isla del Sol is one of the lake's sacred islands, and one of its largest. It sits close to the Bolivian town of Copacabana, to which it is linked by ferry. This photograph is taken from the top, a place of ancient ceremonies. Creation myths are said to have occurred here.

below One Incan myth states that Viracocha, the god of creation, wore the sun as his crown, wept rain and brandished lightning flashes in his hands. He arose from the waters and brought the world into being, flung the glittering stars into the night sky and allowed clouds to run across the blue skies of daytime to dance with the sun. He was worshipped at this site.

above left Villages of reed float on islands of *totora* reed, where the Uros people live. The floating foundation for the village as well as the homes are constructed from the *totora*. There are over 40 of these islands in Lake Titicaca, which are constantly being rebuilt as they rot.

left The *totora* are used to make boats and houses. In addition, the blanched base of the reed is eaten as a useful source of iodine, the upper part is wrapped around areas of pain and the flower is used to make tea.

above Archaeologists found a ruined, pre-Incan temple underneath these waters, thought to date from up to 1,500 years ago. It would have been accessed by the 800-metre (2,625 feet) long causeway which has also been discovered, along with a terrace for arable farming. The temple was huge, measuring 200 meters (656 feet) long by 50 metres (164 feet) wide. The complex is thought to have belonged to the indigenous peoples of the region.

INNER JOURNEYS,
SACRED REALMS

Everyone who seeks a relationship with God will

feel their way according to the traditions formed

within their chosen faith group. And the seeking

involves reflections and inner journeys led by prayer,

meditation and contemplation. Prayer involves a degree

of discourse and has many facets, used according to

need and circumstance. There are specific disciplines

and formalities which offer well trodden paths and

structure. These may be collective or individual,

spoken or silent, formalized or spontaneous.

left Prambanan in Java is a mainly Hindu site, but also accommodates
the Buddhist Candi Plaosan temple complex, shown here. The region
suffered earthquakes during 2006 and repair work is underway to restore
the much-visited, much-loved temples.

Under the umbrella of prayer, worship glorifies God with adoration and thanks, acknowledging Him as the infinite source of goodness and the maker of all that is; repentance is the turning away from sin and asking for forgiveness. To request blessings for another is to make intercession and supplication is when we ask for personal help. Beyond prayer, contemplation is non-discursive and transcendent, a lifting up and letting go, while meditation mulls a subject, perhaps by visualizing a process, need or object. All of these techniques move towards purifying the mind and soul. Everything we look at, feel or sense can be a route into an inner journey, a springboard for a spiritual high or a subtle step towards illumination. And these ineffable spiritual landscapes can only be explained by experience – words fall short.

Within a physical journey, the world immediately around us moves away and seems to slip into the past, yet the end point stays where it is. It is our approach that shortens the distance between us and our destination. As to our inner journeys, God stays the same, ever present within us, but we need to clear away the things that veil our view.

In Shravanabelagola, a city in the Indian state of Karnataka, we learn of an obstacle to inner progress from the Jain figure Bahubali. His pride kept him from reaching enlightenment. Despite standing in meditation for so long that vines grew up around him and ants nested at his feet, his spiritual path was blocked. But he would not be distracted by discomfort and did not move; it was not until he was shocked out of his pride that his eyes were opened and the goal of enlightenment was reached. Now, at a ceremony that comes around every 12 years, pilgrims anoint the head of a sculpture of Bahubali with precious gifts. These become potent with sacred energy, communicable to the pilgrims through physical contact, who thus reap spiritual energy to hasten their own enlightenment. A less tangible manifestation of spiritual aid is found among Zoroastrian believers, who sometimes recite their prayers in arcane holy language, allowing the words to lift the mind into a mystical realm away from the human concept of linguistic meaning. We meet the Zoroastrian community in Chak-Chak, or Pir-e-sabz, where prayer rises through veils of incense, the vibration of holy music and the scents and shimmer of the sacred fire. Here, the flame is seen to embody the creator,

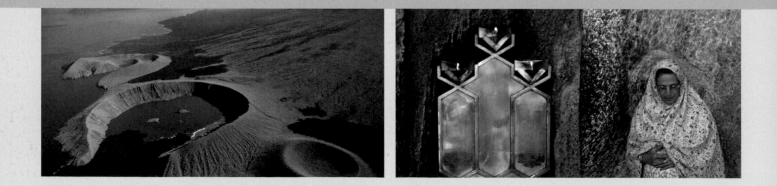

Ahura Mazda, and to aid the visualization of dualism where good and evil are in constant battle; light can spread into darkness, but darkness cannot extinguish the flame. This incandescent visual metaphor is used by many other faiths as an aid to meditation, for example where Christ is seen as the light of the world.

Visual symbols come in infinite form. The natural world is full of them – water, earth, wind and, of course, fire. Among the plant and animal kingdoms, too, there are examples of creation, which, by their beauty, complexity and miraculous interaction with the elements, fill us with sufficient admiration to push us into a state of wonder. The stories which unfold on the Galápagos Islands illustrate this. Here, Darwin was so inspired by the crucible of creation that he published work that still sparks debate about the origins of creation and evolution. And then there are the monarch butterflies, which take a three-month epic journey into the forests of Mexico to help each other pass the bitter winters. These seem to encapsulate sufficient design, wisdom and power to represent all the wonders of the animal kingdom inside their tiny, fragile bodies. Within such creatures

is sufficient glory for a lifetime of meditation and prayer. Our efforts to make sense of sacred realms through spiritual study and exploration can lead us back and forth, twisting and turning as we attempt to find our way, confronting our doubts and trying to clear our vision. The architects who installed labyrinths in great cathedrals such as Amiens in France recognized this inner conundrum. Inspired by the art form's prehistoric templates, they brought the tangled mass of doubt and confusion out of the abstract realm of inner quandary and onto the physical plane. Redesigned along a single path with no false leads, the labyrinth guides its walkers back and forth, round and about until they reach the still point at the middle, the point of stasis.

below left to right Galápagos Islands, Pacific Ocean; Chak-Chak, Yazd Province, India; Candi Sewu Temple at Prambanan, Java; Pine Ridge Reservation, South Dakota, USA.

Shravanabelagola
Karnataka, India

This city in the state of Karnataka takes its name from a sacred 'white pond', called Bel Kola in the Kannada tongue, and its high status as a pilgrim centre has grown from the prodigious number of Jain shrines, along with the gigantic sculpture of Bahubali. Shravanabelagola sits on a pair of mounds, Small Hill and Large Hill, both strewn with temples dating between the ninth and nineteenth centuries. And throughout the whole area are inscriptions scribed onto stone or metal, temples, pillars, exposed rock, curved and flat surfaces. They are written in many scripts and with such flourish that to the untrained eye they may be interpreted as wonderful labyrinthine patterns tumbling across the forms that hold them.

The area has been a pilgrim destination for more than 2,000 years, its former forests furnishing ascetic hermits with food and humble shelter. However, during the tenth century AD, temple building began and this saw the start of more organized pilgrimage. Around

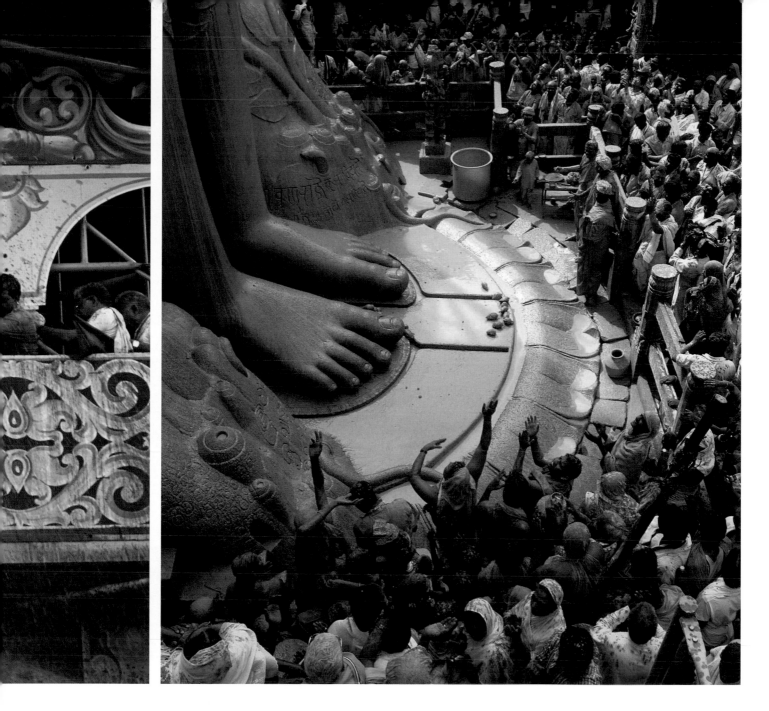

AD 982 a monolith of granite was carved to form Bahubali, standing in meditation; his story is one of self-denial and personal growth. According to Jain scriptures, Bahubali was the youngest of Lord Rishabha's sons, Rishabha being the first Tirthankar – one who leads others towards enlightenment. Bahubali's brother Bharat coveted the younger man's wealth and success and aimed to vanquish him in warfare. But advisors cautioned against this destructive path and instead advocated three rounds of traditional martial combat. When it came to the last challenge, Bahubali, named for the strength of his arms, knew that he could easily win the fist fight and defeat his brother. But in a moment of clarity he saw that such behaviour was against the *ahimsa* (non-violence) their father taught and so surrendered his kingdom to Bharat. Then he opted for the life of a monk. However, this was when Bahubali's inner battle began. A novice monk must bow down to those who have already taken their

vows, but Bahubali was too proud to abase himself and set about meditation on his own terms, with supreme knowledge as his goal. What he could not see was that pride was a huge obstacle blocking his route to enlightenment. Bahubali continued his inner journey

above left This huge statue of Bahubali is honoured in a celebration that takes place every 12 years, when there is advantageous astrological alignment. Over the figure's head is poured a shower of honey, coconut milk, saffron, turmeric petals and water. The colourful, sticky, scented stream runs the full length of the statue, more than 17 metres (56 feet).

above The sculpture's huge feet are firmly planted, and to the left and right are the vine stems that grew around the feet of Bahubali as he was stood rapt in meditation. The figure dates to around AD 978-993, and inscriptions at the base are written in Kannada, Tamil and Marathi.

for so long that vines entwined him and ants nested at his feet, but despite deep meditation, enlightenment would not dawn. Concerned for his wellbeing, the monk's sisters consulted with Rishabha, who suggested that Bahubali must conquer his pride, likening it to an ego the size of an elephant! Surprised at this analogy, Bahubali shed his vanity and was welcomed by his father as one of the enlightened ones, worthy of leading others along the right path.

Once in 12 years, with auspicious astrological alignments, there is an exuberant ceremony to anoint the head of this huge statue of Bahubali; 1,008 pots of milk, honey, sugar cane juice, herbs, saffron and petals are poured over the head of the figure. The run-off collected at Bahubali's feet is potent with spiritual energy aiding inner journeys for those who take it.

right Herbs, spices and liquids are poured from 1,008 vessels, this being an auspicious number, because the digits add up to nine and there are nine stages on the spiritual path. For the same reason there are 108 beads on a prayer *mala*.

left above and below Pilgrims catch the run-off from the sculpture and joyfully anoint themselves with the sacred balm, which is passed around the crowd. This mixture acts as a spiritual salve, aiding progress along the route to inner purity. The colours of saffron and turmeric promote wisdom and nurture the soul.

below On the first day of the festival, pilgrims toil up the hill to where the statue stands. The route is set out to be clear and welcoming, and announces the importance of the occasion. It is traditional to climb the hill barefoot, but those who cannot climb are helped by being carried in chairs, as we can see on the right of the picture.

left Shravanabelagola means 'the monk who lives on the top of the hill'. Thought to be the world's largest monolith, the sheer size of the image allows us to appreciate the calm expression on the sculpture's face.

above Scaffold is erected so that the celebratory pouring may be done efficiently and safely. Each individual makes the most of this rare event (the last Mahamastakabhisheka was in 2006 and the next will not fall until 2018). In Jainism, the purpose of life is to reach *moksa* – release from the cycle of rebirth – and ceremonies such as this help worshippers on their inner journey.

Jaya Sri Maha Bodhi
Anuradhapura, Sri Lanka

The sacred Sri Maha Bodhi is acknowledged as the world's oldest surviving tree, with a lineage that elevates it to yet higher status. For this is the offspring of the original Bodhi Tree that played a role in the Buddha's enlightenment, the awakening of understanding known as Bodhi. The sacred fig tree was brought to Sri Lanka as a cutting around the third century BC from Bodh Gaya in India, and all those accumulated years of reverence have ennobled the tree further. It was planted high upon a terrace, 6.5 metres (21 feet) above the ground and enclosed by a wall not only to enshrine it but to protect it from grazing elephants. A city sprang up around the shrine and this became a religious and political centre, abandoned for a time after invasion, but now ranking as one of Buddhism's holiest pilgrim destinations.

Since very early times, trees have been widely recognized as the dwellings of deities, as bridges between earth and heaven. Offerings of food and riches would be given in the hope that blessings would shower down in return. It is believed that this tree holds unique supernatural powers. These stem from the link with its parent tree and the Buddha's enlightenment, that bolt of sacred energy conducted through a chain of physical contact. At Sri Maha Bodhi there is a cycle of daily and annual rituals to care for the tree, honour its holiness and allow pilgrims to make supplication. Collectively these acts are called Bodhi-Puja. These practical nurturing and routine rituals are carried out by monks or laymen who fully understand that they are, effectively, in the presence of the Buddha. Pilgrims may bow, make offerings and chant at designated stations. Bowing is usually performed thrice: firstly for the Buddha, represented here by the tree; secondly for the Dharma, Buddha's teaching in the physical world; and finally for the Sangha, the community of fellow Buddhists. While making these gestures, it is traditional to place the palms together and perhaps allow them to touch the head, mouth and chest, submitting the mind, speech and heart. Offerings represent gratitude, aid a better rebirth and prepare the mind for meditation. The gifts may be candles, incense, fruit or flowers. Chanting calms the mind and body and brings thoughts to the here and now, channelling awareness into the state of meditation and preparing the way towards that awakening of clarity that is so desired.

right One pilgrim studies a sacred text as shadows lengthen on full moon day, known as Poya Day. To be studying on this sacred ground at this auspicious time increases spiritual lift and deepens understanding. In the background, others sit quietly, removed from the bustle and excitement elsewhere.

Another act of ritual linking with the inner life involves the driving away of evil. If a person is experiencing difficulties it may be due to inauspicious astrological effects. These may be diagnosed through horoscope readings and assuaged by lighting a prescribed number of coconut oil lamps, along with offerings of rice milk, medicinal oils or coins cleansed in saffron water. Together with colourful flags fluttering prayers into the breeze and incense rising heavenward, this is a shrine humming with the sacred vibrations of colour, scent and sound, connecting those senses with our inner visions.

above left Prayer flags are tied around the Bodhi Tree, with every little breeze sending the prayers fluttering through the air. The meaning of the prayer depends upon the symbol, words or mantra it holds, and the colours used to depict them. Colours bear meanings associated with the elements, parts of the body, the emotions and even om or aum, the sound of the universe.

above top It has long been traditional to put aside worldly concerns at full moon, or *poya*, and concentrate instead on spiritual matters. This is what is being observed here in the temple grounds.

above Flowers are among the offerings brought to the Bodhi Tree. The white lotus flower represents spiritual growth, by virtue of its rising above the surface of the water and reaching for the light. Even though its roots are in the mud, the flower remains clean: white symbolizes purity.

Galápagos Islands
Pacific Ocean

In an area of high seismic and volcanic activity, 1,000 kilometres (621 miles) west of Ecuador, three ocean currents collide. This cauldron of creative activity houses the paradise known as the Galápagos Islands. The archipelago is still evolving: the Isle of Isabela was reshaped by volcanic eruption as recently as 2008, while the oldest island is thought to have been formed up to 10 million years ago. Altogether there are 19 islands and over 100 smaller islets and rocky outcrops. The isolation and unparalleled conditions here are what have engendered the area's unique life forms. Several endemic species of finch, the giant saddleback tortoises that lend their Spanish name to the islands, and the land iguanas were among the catalysts for Charles Darwin's theories of natural selection. These findings eventually informed his understanding of evolution and challenged contemporary scientific and religious thinking.

The English naturalist set off in 1831 on a five-year voyage on a ship named *The Beagle*. From Darwin's point of view this would be a serendipitous adventure; he had been invited as a gentleman companion to the captain of an expedition assigned to chart and survey South America; he was also to collect specimens of natural history and investigate the geology of the sites at which they stopped on their way. Throughout the voyage Darwin puzzled over the layers of white seashells compressed in volcanic cliffs high above the ocean and the fossils of unknown animals, mysteries which stirred the young man's inquisitiveness and sparked his creative thinking powers. By the time the expedition reached the Galápagos Islands, Darwin had seen sufficient material to make him question the received notions of scientific theory and natural history that currently prevailed. He was also engaged in thoughts about the shifting land masses he had read of in Charles Lyell's *Principles of Geology* and was forming opinions about the injustice of slavery and the notion that one race could claim superiority over others. All of this material enriched and expanded as the journey continued, eventually distilling to form his understanding of the origins of species and to challenge the paths of scientific and religious concepts of creation. Study and deep questioning eventually resulted in a prodigious number of publications and to this day these stimulate debate

right Craters create an other-worldly landscape on the volcanic Isle of Isabela, the largest in the Galápagos archipelago. Marine and land iguanas play here, as do Galápagos penguins and sea turtles, while tortoises lay their eggs in the soft sands in synchrony with the moon. The island was formed only one million years ago and still has several active volcanoes.

and inner journeys among many who seek to reconcile creation myths with scientific evidence. Darwin's *On the Origin of Species by Means of Natural Selection* was published during 1859 and in some circles there are those who still seek to disprove its contents.

For those to whom the future of the Galápagos Islands is entrusted, there is a need to balance the desires of visitors who come to bask in the beauty of the place with the inevitable environmental impact of an eager tourist industry. The microcosm of evolution and what can be learnt here is so precious and finely balanced that it occupies a physical and metaphorical realm that transcends the boundaries of the marine reserve.

above The island of Santiago, once habituated by buccaneers and used as a stopping-off point for whalers, has quite a long history of human activity. It is now a favourite place for those wishing to study the Galápagos hawks, vermilion flycatchers and other gems of wildlife. Imported goats thrived here and have upset the ecological balance, so steps are being taken to redress the situation.

above Boobies are birds named for their sleepy nature, which allowed them to be captured as they dozed. The blue-footed ones are the most common type found on the Galápagos Islands. They nest in colonies and breed almost continuously.

left Tourists with backpacks climb the volcanic slopes to enjoy the spectacular views and the beautiful flora and fauna. The islands are so remote that the wildlife has never felt threatened enough to fear human company; this unique closeness lends a paradisal quality, which is highly treasured by those who interact with the special creatures found here.

Amiens Cathedral
Amiens, France

The city of Amiens is graced with a cathedral of twelfth-century Gothic splendour. The exterior rises forever heavenwards; with the tip of the spire piercing the sky 113 metres (370 feet) above the ground, it is a perfect pinnacle. Elaborate carvings depict saints and stories to delight the eye and tell of Christ in majesty, the last judgement and the attributes of saints. Buttresses and portals support the imagery like a picture book fanned open, revealing poetry and drama, gospel and parable on every surface. East to west the building stretches for 145 metres (476 feet), accommodating the longest nave (133 metres/ 438 feet) in France. Fire has destroyed the archives which narrated the cathedral's history, but we do know that there has been a church here since the ninth century, a bishopric since the mid-fourth, and that the missionary preacher Fermin was martyred here in AD 303.

On entering the building the visitor is dwarfed by the sculptures piled high in the arched portals, line upon line, like text on a page. Inside the walls, the sacred space opens out and leads the eye up the columns, across the vaulting and back down to floor level where, in 1288, architect Renaud de Cormont laid a labyrinth. This was destroyed around 1825, but replaced 70 years later and now sits amid the geometry of highly patterned tiles. Were it not for the studious tread of those who pace it, it could go unnoticed by visitors whose gaze is captivated by the architectural wonders overhead. Like the columns that take their forms from the sacred forests of our ancestors, labyrinths have their roots in nature and hold a subtle inner function. Sacred geometry is informed by the mathematical ratios found in the natural world. The coil of a shell and the spiral of a pinecone conform to measurable patterns and relate to universal expressions of harmony and proportion. Just as the turn of a growing shoot follows the path of the sun, these designs connect with the cosmos and offer artists and architects a link with the creator's hand and thus a way of infusing space with sacred resonance. To enter the labyrinth allows the traveller to come into that realm. Furthermore, the path is symbolic of our journey through life. Looping and turning, its repetitive line stills the mind and invites a perambulatory meditation. The single track has no false leads and allows no adherent to lose the way. Instead it shepherds the traveller to walk towards the heart of the labyrinth, the resting place at the centre which faces east, the altar and Jerusalem.

At the time of this building's construction, Jerusalem was regarded as a symbol of heaven, and so to walk the labyrinth was to embark on a pilgrimage in miniature, an alternative for those who could not make the longer journey. Some find this experience empties the mind, allowing fresh thoughts to flow in on leaving; for others, it induces deep prayer. Either way, returning to the world represents a new journey.

left Amiens Cathedral welcomes visitors with a breathtaking array of sculptures and carvings, including a Saint Christopher, the patron saint of travellers. The sculptures were originally highly painted in chromatic splendour. The effect of all the external narrative is almost dizzying and prepares the pilgrim for the mesmeric effect of the labyrinth within.

below It is with delight that pilgrims enter the labyrinth. The black and white pattern enhances its geometric effect and makes the path easy to follow and totally absorbing. To enter on the black line at the bottom of this image and walk sunwise is to enter the ancient tradition of aligning oneself to the movement of the sun and stars.

Chak-Chak
Yazd Province, Iran

About 72 kilometres (45 miles) north of Yazd, in the desert of Central Iran, is the country's most sacred Zoroastrian temple and pilgrim destination; it is named Pir-e Sabz, or Chak-Chak, after the drip-drip sound of water. The shrine is high up in a crumbly mountain, which is the scene of a mysterious event. When Arab armies invaded Iran, the ancient Zoroastrian faith and way of life came under threat, and it is said that during AD 652 Nikbanou, one of the daughters of Persian Emperor Yazdegerd III, tried to escape capture and fled into the desert. On arriving here she prayed to God for protection. As the enemy approached, the mountain opened up to enclose and conceal her, and thus she was spared. At the same moment, the mountain wept with the waters that still fall today and mark the site as holy. In this faith fire, sun, earth and water are hallowed elements of creation.

Over time, a sanctuary was established to house a fire temple and the flames that burn within have flickered and sparked for over a thousand years. The chamber walls have been blackened by soot from the blaze of sandalwood and frankincense, enhancing the symbolic contrast between darkness and light. In Zoroastrianism, fire is the paramount sign of Ahura Mazda, or God, his life-giving energy and righteousness. It also represents cosmic order, *asha*, along with the inner light of the individual and the creative spark of all that is.

Every June, thousands of pilgrims come here for an annual festival of worship and fellowship. By tradition, travellers finish their journey on foot, once the shrine is within sight. The terrain is rough, dry and barren, and on leaving the flat plain the track zigzags up the mountain and then gives way to steps as the climb steepens and approaches the brass doors of the fire temple. Sacred music fills the air along with the scent of incense and the endless splash of water. Interweaving, these touch the senses and prepare the pilgrim to receive the numinous, transcendent presence. Around the shrine are antechambers, one of which has a 50-metre (164-foot) deep well. Into this dips a rope, which pilgrims may tie a string around while whispering a prayer, to link it directly with the mountain's holy stream.

Cord is also used as a signal during the initiation ceremony, or Sedreh Pushi. At this, sacred words are read as the child initiate is dressed in a *sedreh*, a pure white linen garment which has a pocket to be filled, symbolically, with good thoughts, good words and good deeds every day. The *sedreh* is then tied with a woollen cord called a *koshti*, indicating that the child is bound to the teachings of Zoroaster.

Away from formal worship, festivities spill into relaxed celebrations, where the constraints of life within this Islamic nation are waived. Wine is shared and women need not wear the veil, so this occasion is a true opportunity to celebrate Zoroastrian tradition and fan the flames of faith.

above Brass doors open onto the fire temple bearing images of Zoroaster, or Zarathustra, the ancient Iranian prophet who lends his name to the Zoroastrian faith. It was he who first taught the concept of individual judgement, and thus the notions of heaven and hell.

right above Within the fire temple there is time for individual prayer and communal worship. Dating back to the sixth century BC, Zoroastrianism is thought to be the world's oldest monotheistic faith.

right below Around the altar in the fire temple, worshippers recite their prayers five times daily and read from the sacred texts. The flames, which must be kept burning with sandalwood and frankincense, symbolize the inner light which burns within each of God's people.

Prambanan

Java, Indonesia

Also known as Loro Jonggrang, Prambanan is a complex of shrines clustered around three glorious temples dedicated to the Hindu deities Brahma, Vishnu and Shiva. Within this Trimurti, or 'three forms', Brahma embodies the passion that creates, Vishnu manifests the goodness which maintains balance, and Shiva the fire which destroys. The temples were certainly built with passion. They are decorated with ornament, story and ingenuity. And they have kept a large degree of balance, considering the destructive forces that have shaken their foundations, most recently an earthquake during 2006.

Built in the tenth century, the temples rise from the surrounding parkland and stand 47 metres (154 feet) high, glorifying the narratives they bear and the deities they honour. The main temples stand upon a square, elevated platform, enclosed by walls with square gates at each of the cardinal points. The Brahma, Vishnu and Shiva temples face the rising sun and each has a smaller, counterpart temple of its respective vahana. In mythology, a vahana acts as an attribute or vehicle, sometimes called a mount.

The initial impact of the complex is one of awe generated by the scale and grandeur. The confidence of the structures speaks of authority, the fantastic elaboration of some other realm. To some degree there is always an aspect of this when visiting great architecture, but that first impact gently gives way to looking more closely and absorbing detail, and detail is something that this site has on a grand scale.

The Shiva temple, being the largest, is also distinguished by having an entrance on each side, leading to the inner chambers which house some remarkable sculptures, although these have not always been accessible since the earthquake. The outside is encrusted with a mesmeric display of carvings telling the tale of the Sanskrit epic *Ramayana*. These carvings are enthralling in their craftsmanship and styling, their narrative skill, and the way they reach across time with their eternal meaning. Detail here is realistic, expressive and wonderful. Together these aspects fuse with the overall structure to lead the eye into mystical musings. It is said that the temples were built by magic. Loro Jonggrang was the daughter of the giant king

Ratu Baka (known as the king of death), and the handsome Bandung Bandawasa desired her hand in marriage. But the princess did not wish to give herself to him and formed a plan to thwart him. She said that if he could build 1,000 temples before the next daybreak, she would be his bride. Unbeknown to Loro Jonggrang, her would-be suitor had supernatural allies. He called on genies and the temples were built apace. When they reached the 999th temple, the princess knew she needed to outwit him once again. So she instructed her servants to make the sounds of cooking and bustling that go with morning routine. This set the cocks crowing and the genies fled the impending dawn. On realizing what had happened, Bandung Bandawasa flew into a rage and cursed Loro Jonggrang. She was turned to stone, and there she stands within the Shiva temple. Yet tourists may think that Durga, the goddess of darkness and wife of Shiva, is the figure they see, for she has taken that form. The shrine of Durga is also called the 'temple of the slender virgin' in reference to Loro Jonggrang.

previous page (left) The temple walls are lovingly worked with friezes relating scenes from the *Ramayana* and the lives of the deities. Here we see a figure whose deep meditation is aided by prayer beads. Note the skill and detail in the carving, which has survived with remarkable clarity from the tenth century.

previous page (right) Shiva, Vishnu and Brahma are the main Hindu deities honoured at this temple complex, although Prambanan also accommodates Candi Sewu, a Buddhist temple. It is easy to spot the difference in architectural styles, with the Buddhist construction being more rounded. What is less clear is the relationship the two faith groups enjoyed as the site was being developed.

left The glorious architecture reaches skyward in elongated pyramidal form, resembling at once both towering mountains and the cut facets of gemstones. It is wonderful to visualize the building process and to marvel at the ingenuity that went into conceiving the overall plan, the strength that sustained that vision, and the skill that ensured that function and finish would serve glorious worship.

right The earthquake which shook the region during 2006 caused considerable damage with its 6.4 magnitude, and we can see that this shrine to Brahma has been shaken to the core. Repair work is underway, although access is limited around some of the structural damage.

The Shrine of Fátima
Fátima, Portugal

During the months of May to October each year the town of Fátima is thronged with pilgrims who come to connect with the visions of the Virgin Mary, experienced by three shepherd children during 1917. It was on the thirteenth day of each of those six months that Lucia, Francisco and Jacinta saw a figure who introduced herself as the Lady of the Rosary. But the children not only saw the Virgin, they also engaged in conversation and received instructions, all at Cova da Iria, a little way from the town of Fátima. The recurrent theme of the meetings was that they should promote the use of the rosary as a route to personal and global peace. A rosary is a set of prayer beads, a tactile aid to deepen prayer through meditation; each bead is touched in turn and has a specific prayer associated with it, according to its position and size within the loop. The message held deep resonance at that time of the First World War.

On October 13 of that same year, the last vision occurred. A crowd of 70,000 people had gathered, including journalists, sceptics and zealous believers. All were eagerly anticipating another mystical event; many hoped to be touched by the gift of healing. The weather was vile, with a black sky and driving rain, but all at once the sun burst through the clouds and shone with incredible radiance. Witnesses said that the solar disc broke into a spinning whorl of colours, illuminating all it touched with the same glow. Then the sky went black for several minutes, after which the sun appeared to plunge towards the earth and then return to its normal appearance and position. A journalist who had previously doubted the children's accounts reported this phenomenon with credible conviction, though his photographer captured nothing more than the astonished faces of the witnesses. Furthermore, other members of the crowd made statements confirming the report, including some who had previously mocked the 'simpletons' for believing the children's stories. Reasonable people well away from the village recounted seeing the same event at the same time, thus excluding the possibility of mass hysteria among the crowd as a possible explanation for what was claimed.

A chapel was built to mark the site of the apparitions, but this was destroyed with dynamite by anti-Catholic activists in 1922; by luck or by providence, the figure of the Lady of the Rosary, carved according to the children's direction, was not inside at the time. Enshrined, this statue (Our Lady of Fátima) now marks the site of the manifestations, and is visited by four million visitors each year. Pilgrims from across the globe arrive on the 12th day of the month and a formal cycle of services and processions begins. The ritual of the International Rosary allows the pilgrims' words to extend from the realm of meditation and commune with those around them, regardless of their nationality. Thus the act is not about language so much as connecting with God's people and, ultimately, with the divine.

left above The statue of Virgin Mary during a procession to celebrate the 90th anniversary of the first apparition to three children in 1917.

left below The Basilica of Our Lady of Fátima is built on the site of the children's vision, which was said to be brighter than the sun. Construction of the central tower, which is over 65 metres (195 feet) high, began in 1928.

below Thousands of pilgrims, holding candles, surround the statue of Our Lady of Fátima. This candlelight procession traditionally takes place at the Fátima Sanctuary.

The Pine Ridge Reservation
South Dakota, USA

The Pine Ridge Reservation is an Oglala Sioux reservation in South Dakota. The conditions here are extreme, with bitter winters and hot summers. Fire, flood and tornados are not unusual and so the elements are very much a part of everyday life in this 8,000-square kilometre (3,089-square mile) wilderness. During the winter months, travel is limited. People here rely on their own resources and work hard to sustain their cultural identity and self-sufficiency. Spirituality is closely linked to respect for creation, and with the gifts sent by the Great Spirit, who is also known as Waken Tanka.

Oglala Sioux devotion is rich in symbol and ceremony, marking rites of passage and honouring nature. Among the rites is the vision quest, also known as 'crying for a vision' or 'lamenting'. This spiritual journey forms bonds between the traveller and all of creation; it can be taken by anyone, but most often by a young man wanting to find direction in life. Or it may be embarked upon to ask for another's healing, to give thanks for a blessing or just to achieve oneness with creation. The person wishing to seek a vision, the 'lamenter', takes a filled pipe to a holy man and asks for his help. The pipe is deeply symbolic and to smoke it is to unite with the universe. The holy man invokes the elements of creation, the natural world and the ancestors, and offers the pipe in the six directions, that is the cardinal points (north, south, east, west), heaven and earth. After this an inipi, or sweat lodge, is built, and used for a purification ceremony in preparation for divine intervention and the Great Spirit's blessing. The space is heated with hot stones; sage and cedar give off resinous vapours while symbolic objects and sacred earth are purified, and the holy man offers prayers. The pipe is then sealed and the lamenter, crying to the Great Spirit, sets off up the mountain, where he will spend the next few days pacing north, south, east and west between four poles set to mark the cardinal points. Walking in this way forms the shape of a cross, meaning that he is constantly returning to the centre, the place of power, the seat of the Great Spirit to whom we must all return.

In the course of this pacing the lamenter prays and is constantly alert for a messenger sent by the Great Spirit. The messenger may take the form of any living creature. During the whole ceremony, the lamenter neither eats nor drinks. He may sleep, because dreams often hold the sought-after visions. The quest ends when the holy man and his helper come to fetch the lamenter down from the mountain. The group returns to the inipi for a further ceremony, during which the lamenter describes his experience and new understanding while the holy man gives thanks. Emerging from the darkness of the Inipi is a symbolic entry into the realm of the Great Spirit – the door faces east, the direction of the light of wisdom.

left Pine forests are broken by the bare rock face of a quarry. Look closer and you will see a human face emerging. This work in progress is a memorial to Crazy Horse, leader of the Oglala Sioux, who fought the government in their struggle to preserve their way of life and traditional values.

above This memorial to Crazy Horse in the Black Hills of Dakota stands in proud profile against the blue sky, a fitting tribute to an honoured leader. The work was begun in 1948 by the US sculptor Korczak Ziolkowski at the request of Chief Henry Standing Bear. The reservation is noted for its natural beauty and includes pine forests, grassy plains and desert.

above Within a vision quest natural beings and manmade objects take on great significance. Here we see aspects of the eagle and buffalo represented in wing and skull. The eagle, Wambli Galeska, sees all by flying higher than any other being. His wing feathers represent the sun's rays. The buffalo, Tatanka, supplies so many needs that it represents the universe.

above According to Black Elk, a famous Oglala Sioux holy man, when the morning sun shines upon the world we are blessed by the grace of the Great Spirit and enlightened. Our vision becomes a sacred journey through the eye of the heart. This woman holds her hands up to that grace as she greets the day.

right The Black Hills Stream winds through the landscape, where the sacred Mother Earth produces all that grows, and the Grandmother aspect is the potential that makes growth possible.

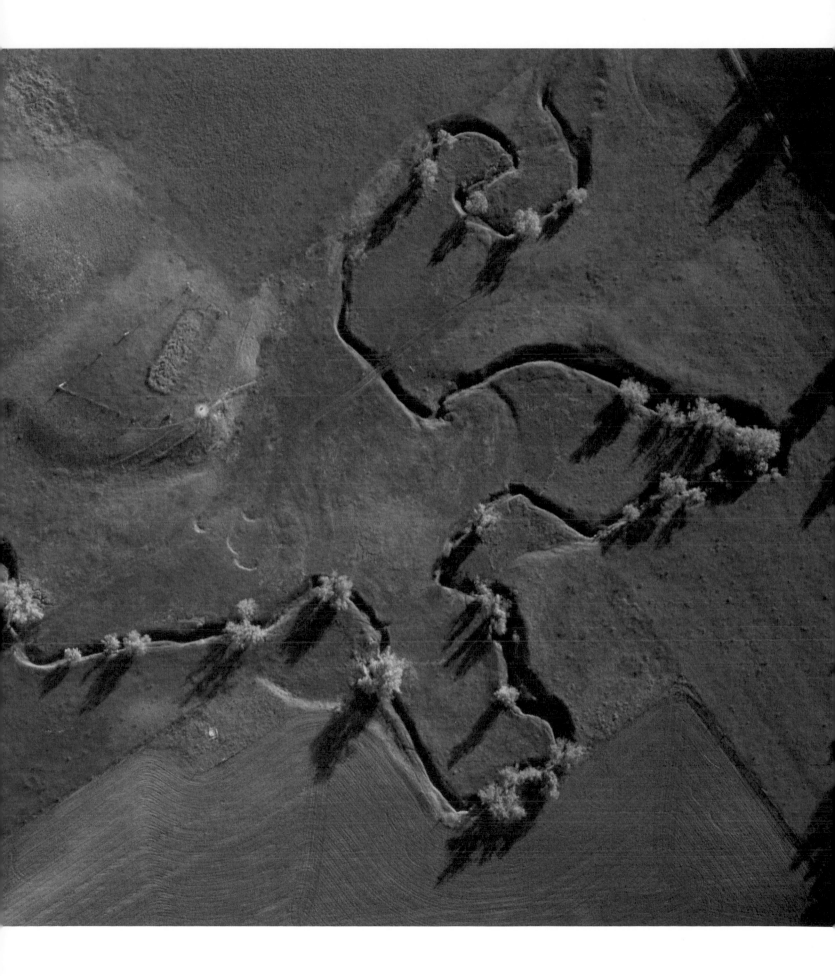

Peterborough Petroglyphs
Ontario, Canada

Situated northeast of Peterborough, Ontario, is the 20-square kilometre (8-square mile) provincial park, known for its ancient rock carvings. There is some dispute about the official age of the petroglyphs (rock scribings) and their makers; the oldest estimate is that they date to the fourth millennium BC and represent images of European influence. However, the most widely accepted theory is that they were made by the aboriginal First Nations people about 1,000 years ago.

The stone carvings offer us insights into the spiritual awareness of the aboriginal people here, and their relationship with the Great Spirit, sought through mysticism. The setting for these is among the forests, lakes and marshes, which are in themselves a store of great transcendent beauty, a landscape which has no doubt fed the imagination and fuelled thoughts of the inner life since man first set foot here. Known as the teaching rocks, or Kinomagewapkong, by local Indians, these mysterious figures are cut into a huge slab of crystalline marble. An unclaimed, clear, flat surface is an open invitation to anyone with an artistic mind; the urge to make marks on a surface irresistible. While images often take a formalized pictorial space in ancient art, showing perhaps sky, earth and underworld, here there is no such structure. Creatures of the air, land and sea intermingle with elongated humanoid cyclopean figures, all inhabiting the same plane, and with no clear orientation as to up or down.

However, while at first glimpse the 900 or so carvings appear randomly placed, there are clues as to the reasons for this choice of location. Throughout the world and across the ages, rock art has been made at places of energy or with connection to other realms: springs, caves, mountain tops, waterfalls and so on. Historically, these are the places where worship and ritual have been focused. And here, across this surface the figures are placed in accordance with that system, around the rock's hollows, fissures and grooves. But this slab holds another force of mystery that would have drawn people's awe – at certain times, the rock sings and chatters with human-sounding noises. Emanating from the fissures, one of which is 5 metres (16 feet) deep in places, is the babble of an underground stream, which swells when the water table is high.

In traditional Indian spirituality, spirits dwell in cliffs, rocks and caves. It is the shaman's job to commune with them, find out about the sacred realms they inhabit, and learn from them. Thus these teaching rocks could offer insights for the holy man and no doubt played a part in traditional vision quests. The rocks themselves are sacred, representing the indestructible nature of the Great Spirit and symbolizing the earth, bearer of worldly sustenance. They are no longer actively used for formal worship, although the site is regarded as sacred by many who are of First Nation descent. And while some come here and find a place of recreation and cultural curiosity, others journey as pilgrims with due reverence for the Great Spirit's presence in all that is around them, and for His powers of re-creation.

left Among the beautiful forests of the Petroglyphs Provincial Park lie the quietly beguiling figures on the crystalline marble Teaching Rocks. The figures represent beings from this world and some other, inner realm accessible only to the shaman.

right above and below The drawings are scribed into the surface of the rock and cluster around the naturally-occurring features of its surface, particularly at places where the rocks 'sing'. However, the characters are not formalized into any particular orientation of up, down or perspectival distance. Rather, they appear to have been randomly sprinkled across the surface of the rock, and are perhaps meant to be read from various viewpoints above ground level, in the domain of the Great Spirit.

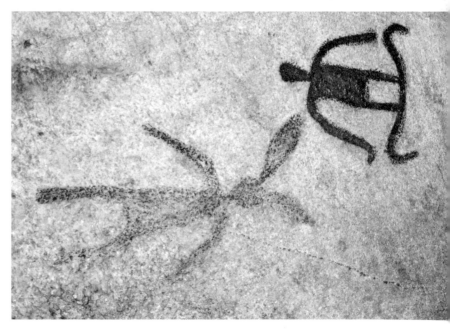

Lumbini
Nepal

In Sanskrit, the liturgical language of many Indian religions, Lumbini means 'the lovely'. Situated in the town of Kapilavastu, close to the Indian border, it is the honoured birthplace of the Buddha. While many people know that the Buddha reached enlightenment beneath the distant pipal tree that shot forth on the day of his birth, it is not so widely known that he was also born beneath the boughs of a tree. When her birth pains began that day in 623 BC, his mother Queen Maya went to a grove of trees. She grasped a teak branch in her right hand and the baby Prince Siddhartha emerged from her right side. Tradition says that at once he uttered that this would be his final rebirth, then took seven steps, leaving a lotus flower in each footprint. Finally he stopped and stood with one hand pointing to heaven, the other to the earth.

This extraordinary tale speaks of sacred journeys. First, the baby destined to become the Buddha was acknowledging the cyclical nature of his spiritual passage, through which he had been reborn. He was also predicting his arrival at the state of final liberation, nirvana, in this new lifetime. The second sign was contained within the seven steps and lotus flowers. The steps signify each direction: the four cardinal points and heaven, earth and here, where we stand. The lotus flower is a symbol of spiritual purity, the essence

of his leadership along the Noble Eightfold Path. This is the course that followers of Buddhism still tread. These eight disciplines steer a righteous route and act as moral guidelines. Pilgrims come to Lumbini to feel his nascent presence in the peaceful sacred garden and to worship in the Maya Devi Temple. They may also reflect around the Pushkarni Pool, wherein Queen Maya bathed before giving birth, and in which her newborn child was dipped.

There is also the Ashoka Pillar, one of many such monuments which Emperor Ashoka (304–232 BC) erected as he strove to spread the Buddha's teaching. The former warrior was ashamed of the lives lost and wasted in his military campaigns, and converted to Buddhism with such zeal that many were drawn to follow. Not content to simply lead by domestic example, he ruled his empire according to Buddhist precepts and sent emissaries on missionary expeditions to lands far beyond his own. On his own proselytizing journeys he established pillars such as the Ashoka one bearing proclamations, heralding Buddhist philosophy for all to see and learn from. But perhaps the most far-reaching of the journeys relating to Lumbini are the ones taken quietly, within its walls. Beyond the ancient monuments is an extensive international monastic zone reserved for different branches of the Theravada and

Mahayana Buddhist traditions. There are also research facilities, an auditorium and a library, which represent a long-term commitment to inquiry, learning and understanding. This means that those who study with Right Effort, Right Mindfulness and Right Concentration (three components of the Eightfold Path) may then leave equipped with sure footsteps along the well-mapped route.

above left Lumbini is the Buddha's birthplace. Named Prince Siddhartha at birth, he sprang from his mother's side within a grove of trees here, one full moon day. The site has long been a place in which to devote oneself to the great man's philosophy. Today the archaeological remains form a focal point to pilgrimage in his honour.

above Queen Maya is said to have bathed in this pool before giving birth to Prince Siddhartha. It is also believed that he had his first bath here shortly after coming into the world. Today the site is run by monks and nuns who lead faithful pilgrims into peaceful lives full of compassion, through their teaching, chanting and all-inclusive lifestyles.

Monarch Butterfly Reserve
Michoacan, Mexico

Every winter clouds of monarch butterflies (*danaus plexippus*) make their way to the forests on the volcanic belt 100 kilometres (62 miles) north of Mexico City. This is the Santuario de la Mariposa Monarca, the Monarch Butterfly Reserve. The monarchs come to spend the winter bunched together in the branches of the sacred oyamel fir trees, *abies religiosa*. And they come in their millions. Cloud upon cloud of these creatures, orange and brown-black, flecked with white spots, they fill the skies like tiny airborne stained-glass windows. One by one they cling to the trees and cluster together. They are fragile, impossibly light and delicate, yet their collective weight bends the branches as they cling on, pressed against the winter cold. These ephemeral beings have come from as far away as eastern Canada, on an eight-month journey of 3,200 kilometres (1,988 miles). They will set off north again when the spring comes.

Packed inside their tiny bodies is the power and wisdom that will fuel and guide that epic venture. But no one knows how the butterflies plot their course. Whether it be solar compass, magnetic field or some arcane force we have yet to recognize, the creatures guard their secret skill. Here then is a symbol of the maker's might. Contained within each insect is a navigational system we cannot see or comprehend, driven by an instinct we cannot imagine, and with a value we cannot quantify. Yet value them we do. Their sense of purpose and endurance, their grandeur and majesty, and their mutual support against the harsh winter weather is nothing short of miraculous. It kindles our sense of awe and helps us to grasp something of the wonder, depth and detail of the natural world. Butterflies are weighty in their meaning too. As the life cycle passes from egg to caterpillar to pupa, and then finally to that fluttering burst of colour and beauty, it symbolizes life, death and resurrection, or repeated rebirth, liberation and new beginnings, according to belief.

But what of these butterflies and their winter retreat in Mexico? The trees they favour only grow at high altitude, between 2,400 and 3,600 metres (7,874 and 11,811 feet), and their distribution is limited. Furthermore, agriculture, housing and the timber trade are taking their toll, and thus the monarchs are critically endangered. But this forest biosphere of 91,800 square kilometres (35,444 square miles) is now protected to sustain the butterflies' future. A side effect of this is that it safeguards the habitats of all of the species dependent upon the forests here. In the soil beneath the roots, across the forest floor, in the bark, upon the leaves and along to the cruciform tips that give the sacred oyamel fir its name, are flora and fauna, known and unknown but each with a place in creation. And in supporting these, we all benefit.

above The monarch butterflies, *danaus plexippus*, cluster together to survive the harsh winter conditions of the Monarch Butterfly Reserve forests, north of Mexico City. The temperature can sink to –18°C (0°F), but together they will survive and fly back north when spring comes.

right Another defence mechanism the butterflies have developed is to eat milkweed, which renders them poisonous to predators. Their bright colouration and pattern announce this as a flash of colour-coded warning. And while we see them as joyful displays of delicate beauty, their tough lifestyle proves their resilience. Furthermore, they have navigational methods which defy our understanding.

left The life cycle of butterflies is used in many cultures to symbolize life, death and resurrection, or rebirth, and as such is a favourite motif in the visual arts and literature. Pictured here, tucked close together in organized fashion, they look like a masterpiece of packaging or pattern-making.

above It is enchanting to be among a cloud of butterflies, but few of us get to be close to such numbers at one time. Fluttering through sunlight, their wings create a display of transcendent colour reminiscent of stained glass windows in a forest-inspired cathedral.

Isle of Iona
Inner Hebrides, Scotland

It was AD 563 when the prince-priest Columba turned his back on Ireland and his troubles. With 12 companions he crossed the sea in a wicker-ribbed, skin-clad boat called a *currach* to the foam-fringed island of Iona. Bronze Age settlers buried their dead here, and tradition claims that kings from Norway, Ireland and Scotland repose in the burial mound called Reilig Odhrain, confirming this as holy ground. Columba's party soon established a Celtic church and monastic community on Iona, which became the base from

which Christianity reached onto the Scottish mainland and into northern England. It is said that when Columba and his men called upon King Bude, the king declined an audience and had the royal doors bolted. Undaunted, Columba made the sign of the cross in front of the door, which flew open and the monks marched in. This simple miracle convinced the king of Columba's God-given authority; he converted to Christianity, and many followed his lead.

When not evangelizing, Columba returned to Iona, where innumerable followers sought him out – and so a tradition of visiting the island for spiritual journeys began. Life in the monastery was austere and disciplined; the Abbot Adamnan (AD 624–704) records that Columba slept on a stone flag with a stone pillow, but this did not stop him from travelling to the heights of spiritual delight. On the remote hill that was his for private prayer and contemplation, he saw angels, clear and certain. And angels marked the ascension of his

below Iona's first sixth-century monastery was made from wattle and daub. Replaced about 600 years later with a stone building, it has been altered and adapted as needs have evolved. Twentieth-century restoration has made it fit for modern purposes and ready to withstand the windswept location. This place of numinous beauty draws pilgrims from across the world.

soul in AD 597; at the hour of Columba's death, a monk in Ireland was given a vision of Iona and the skies above it, resplendent with the brilliance of angels, the air vibrant with their song and chant. Elsewhere, at the same time, a group of fishermen was dazzled by a pillar of fire illuminating the heavens as brightly as the summer sun. These signs confirmed that Columba was truly honoured for all eternity. Thus his zealous disciples were eager to carry his work forward and face the pagans and druids who stood in opposition. Over time the monks' creative skills were honed, with scribes and sculptors working glorious manuscripts, Celtic crosses and other art forms to the glory of God. But Viking raiders first struck during AD 806 and much of the monks' making was lost.

A Benedictine abbey was founded in 1200, remains of which are still visible in the restored building. Today there is a thriving religious life on Iona. During 1938 Scottish soldier and clergyman George MacLeod (1895–1991) founded the Iona Community for people from a variety of Christian traditions who seek to discover news ways of living out the gospel of Christ, based on the island's Celtic heritage, yet fit for a changing world. There are residential facilities for those who stay and programmes of events for those who seek to broaden their faith and deepen their devotion. The raw beauty of the island provides a constant connection with the closeness of nature and the divine, which spoke to Saint Columba and still reaches those who allow the silver sands and sparkling spume to touch their souls.

above left and right There are fine examples of art, literature and craftwork to be found on Iona, as illustrated by these figures and the cross of Saint John. The amount of activity and its impact on visitors' lives is far-reaching, involving people from all backgrounds.

right Saint Columba's Bay is said to be where Columba and his party landed on arrival from Ireland. That was in AD 563, and the work that they instigated is still having remarkable effects upon the world and on the people who come here. The striking beauty, quiet and calm of the island is conducive to the change of pace needed to allow thinking to deepen and faith to flourish.

ARRIVALS AND RITUALS

The etymology of the word 'arrival' takes us to the meaning 'come to land' or 'touch the shore', but there is also the sense of reaching a state of mind, a conclusion. Therefore at the end of a journey we are at once in a new physical and metaphysical place. The act of bodily moving towards a pilgrim destination is to prepare mentally and spiritually for arrival. Reaching is a part of that, it implies deliberately extending towards contact. So, ideally, the traveller is fully engaged and present in every respect, having moved, prepared and finally stopped.

left Two lion statues mark arrival at the main gate of the Konark Sun Temple in India. The thirteenth-century temple is dedicated to the sun god Surya, and it represents a massive chariot, originally with 24 wheels and a team of horses.

The cessation of the journey can lead to further transition though, through the acts of ceremony and ritual. Each August sees thousands of people from diverse backgrounds come to Hiroshima Peace Memorial Park to honour the victims of the world's first atomic bomb. Acts of dedication, sounds and words ensure that the gravity of that occasion is met by a suitable response. The shockwaves from the explosion still reverberate but are mitigated somewhat by the determination of those who energetically seek to make sure it does not recur. Their pledge to campaign for nuclear disarmament is to transform a tragic situation into a beacon of hope for the future, and so the purpose of the ceremonies and the crusade for peace is to heal and reassure.

At Kandy in Sri Lanka, the Buddhist Procession of the Tooth is more celebratory, devoted to a relic and its power. Here, the 15-day festival is loud and ebullient, full of apotropaic fire, colour and display. This party atmosphere is also present in Jani celebrations in Latvia, where the summer solstice is celebrated around an overnight fire, with special food, drink and song reserved for the occasion. The natural landscape is the temple, and trees are the columns which link earth to sky. At Stonehenge on the same night, druids and pagans wait to greet the morning sun as it brushes the stones with the first rays of its longest day. This temple-monument has seen ceremonies unknown to us, but it marks sun and moonlight, upon which we are all dependent, and the cycles to which we have ever linked our own rhythms.

Taizé is a place where people gather to spend time learning to be pilgrims when they leave. In that respect, the point of arrival is the place from which they reach towards the future with open hearts. They prepare for sharing God's light and love with those around them in everyday situations. And in many ways this is the whole point of pilgrimage. Arrival is not about having completed something, then going back to the old ways. It is a search for transformation and in many cases, a quest for healing or forgiveness. Repentance is the act of turning away from sin and moving off in a new direction, a springing point for new life. By definition, then, there must

be a pause, forgiveness sought and a new path taken. This is publicly and dramatically expressed in Seville where we see the penitents move through Holy Week in extraordinary ritual, seeking God's forgiveness of their sins. Here fasting and humility are preparation for spiritual cleansing in the build-up to the tremendous celebration of Easter. This occasion runs concurrently with the journey to Lindisfarne by pilgrims who walk in the same tradition but over a longer distance. In each case the pilgrims' return to the world is illuminated by God's love expressed through Christ's death and resurrection. People are strengthened and enriched by what they have seen and shared.

In Istanbul the faithful arrive at the Sultan Ahmed Mosque for a period of fasting and prayer during the final 10 days of Ramadan. This allows the pilgrims to be present for the mystical Night of Power, away from the world's temptations and absorbed in study with the support of others. The fast is broken by feasting on the day that the new moon's crescent rises with the sun. At this point, those who have been

within the mosque must adjust again to life outside, its noise, demands and patterns. If arrival is about stepping into a new place, then ritual may be described as reaching out to make contact with God through measured actions, a mindful and ceremonial observance, directed towards the Creator. Ritual acts are inevitably imprinted upon those who open themselves, an impact the pilgrim will cherish. What each one feels on returning to the world varies enormously, and there are as many reasons and results as there are journeys. But the results don't all blossom together. Over time and with reflection, things learned, seen and heard will fall into place, their significance being realized when the time is right and the light dawns.

below left to right The Temple of the Tooth, Kandy, Sri Lanka; Holy Week, Seville, Spain; the Konark Sun Temple, Orissa, India; the Sultan Ahmed Mosque, Istanbul, Turkey.

Potala Palace and Jokhang Temple
Lhasa, Tibet

Lhasa, meaning 'place of the gods', is also known as the Sunlit City for the many hours of sunshine it enjoys each year. It sits in a basin encircled by mountains and skirted by the Kyi Chu River. Potala Palace was named by the fifth Dalai Lama, the title coming from Potalaka, the paradise of Avalokiteshvara, the figure celebrated for his supreme compassion. Its design envisions the paradise known in the *sutras* (the Buddhist texts) as 'pure land'.

It is Avalokiteshvara who, among his other roles, helps the dead to enter this faraway realm, a resting place for the faithful to enjoy before moving on to the fulfilment that is nirvana. The living faithful may visit Pure Land in their meditations, or turn prayer wheels lined with mantras. These spinning sacred syllables smooth the way; each rotation sends invocations out to the cosmos with rhythmic resonance.

Since 1642 the palace has been the official residence of the Dalai Lama, head of state and spiritual leader of the people of Tibet. However, in 1959 the current and 14th manifestation of this authority took flight from Chinese invasion and found political asylum in India, where he still lives in exile. The palace awaits his homecoming when better times return. It is renowned as a jewel of cultural wealth and beauty and for auspicious sites such as the ceremonial hall, wherein Dalai

Lamas ascend the throne. In the stupa-tomb chapels rest the relics of many former Dalai Lamas, the sequential incarnations of the Buddha of Compassion, going back to Avalokiteshvara himself. The esteem in which those great men are held is expressed through ritual devotion and lavish ornamentation; jewels, pearls and precious metals stud the surfaces of their tombs, where such transcendent beauty is a joyful celebration of lives well lived for the salvation of others.

Away from the palace stands the Jokhang Temple, one of Buddhism's most sacred prayer sites, and the holiest in Tibet. This was founded in the seventh century by King Songsten Gampo, whose Chinese and Nepalese wives are credited with bringing Buddhism to the country. Arrival here is an opportunity to accumulate good karma through *puja* – worship and offerings to the gods. Pilgrims approach the temple in reverent devotion, standing, stepping and prostrating themselves as they ritually inch forward. Arrival here symbolizes emergence from the darkness of ignorance into the realm of enlightenment. To honour the eighth-century golden statue of the Jowo Shakyamuni Buddha, housed within, is the pilgrims' goal. It is the most venerated image for Tibetan Buddhists and sits in lamp-lit splendour within the main hall of the temple. Here pilgrims feed

left The Potala Palace rises as a harmonious extension of the ground on which it stands. The mountain is the palace and the palace is the mountain; the one designed in respectful harmony with the peak, which ever anticipated its arrival.

below Yak butter lamps are filled at Jokhang Temple. Lamplight transcends darkness and lifts concentration towards enlightenment. While the monks supply and arrange the lamps, pilgrims gain merit with offerings of fuel. An extension of this is to brings gifts for the monks, in thanks for their prayers.

the flickering flames with butter and touch their heads to the statue; thus his gleaming energy spills into their mindfulness and his blessing nourishes their spirits. In return, the pilgrims' chanting vibrates the air with om, the first and sacred song of the universe that graces prayer and mantra. The warm syrupy sounds flow into one long harmony, which binds together all that is, within earth, air and heaven.

above Crowds of pilgrims of all ages come daily to view the palace, which has over 1,000 rooms, 10 times as many shrines and covers 13 storeys. Pilgrims move clockwise through the building, never standing on a threshold. The palace was built as the residence of the Dalai Lama, now in exile in India.

right Within these cylinders are mantras, rolled in scrolls for pilgrims to spin as they pass. This motion activates the prayer, sending its energies and meaning out to the cosmos. The method enables those who cannot read to utter prayers otherwise beyond their grasp. In addition to the inner words, the prayer wheel may be embossed with sacred words.

below Monks shade themselves with parasols, practical objects which also carry symbolic meaning. They represent the dome of the sky and cast protective shade. In this country, the material and decoration of the parasol bear significance, according to the person's status. Thus the Dalai Lama is entitled to silk, as a religious leader, while peacock feathers mark his secular authority.

The Temple and Procession of the Tooth
Kandy, Sri Lanka

Lush with verdant hills, spice crops and tea plantations, Kandy sits high above the tropical heat of Sri Lanka's lower regions, and its monsoon rains are drained by the majestic Mahaweli River. The region is picturesque, and abundant with nature's gifts. Kandy is the English name for Maha Nuvara, or Senkadagalapura. It was the last capital of the Sinhala Kings and is the home of the Temple of the Tooth.

It is said that the Buddha came to Sri Lanka at least three times during his final incarnation, and Buddhism has been practised here for at least 2,000 years. The Dalada Maligawa, or Temple of the Tooth, is a most auspicious pilgrim destination and site of vibrant celebration, whose story begins in India. When the Buddha arrived at his ultimate nirvana, parinirvana, and left forever the cycle of rebirth, he lay down between two trees in Kushinagar and died.

left and below The Procession of the Tooth is a 10-day celebration for Buddhists who come to honour the sacred relic, represented by a casket carried on the back of a royal male elephant. Other elephants dressed in symbolic finery accompany the casket, while flaming torches ward off evil. Dancers, musicians and drummers celebrate with their expressive art forms.

But someone took a tooth from his funeral pyre, a relic picked from the mouth of wisdom. When war erupted in India during the fourth century AD, King Guhasiva sent his daughter Hemamali to the King of Lanka, with the tooth for safekeeping. Princess Hemamali hid the tooth in her hair, then stole away as Hindu armies sacked her father's kingdom. Once in the safety of its new home, the relic was cushioned and kept in a nest of caskets, enshrined for devotion and special occasions. When the royal party came to Kandy, a temple was built to house and honour the tooth, and it has survived repeated war and attempted theft; it was believed that whoever held the tooth was ordained to rule the land. It now enjoys ceremonial status, though it never leaves the temple.

As an act of veneration pilgrims visit this shrine throughout the year, bringing lotus flowers and prayers. But the most significant time to come is during the Esala Perahera festival. Many devotees aim to arrive in time for this, the Procession of the Tooth. It first began during the eighteenth century, and now runs for 10 days around the time of the full moon in July or August. A casket representing the tooth is carried on the back of a royal male elephant, and surrounded by scores of other elephants bedecked

in finery. All around them flaming torches ward off evil, while dancers, musicians and drummers celebrate the relic with their expressive art forms. In all, about 1,000 people are involved in the festival, with about 200,000 attending, making this one of the world's largest Buddhist festivals. Many of the performers, officials and pilgrims dress in white for this occasion. White is the colour of learning, transforming ignorance into wisdom. The elephants have sacred symbolism too. The Buddha was an elephant in several of his incarnations, and a white one visited his mother around the time of his conception. The elephants are dressed in gowns of red, the life force colour of blood and preservation. Embellishments of white lotus flowers denote spiritual purity, recognized down the ages, in the Buddha of Compassion.

above left Children cool themselves by a fountain at Sri Dalada Maligawa, the official name of the Temple of the Tooth. It is thought that the sacred tooth has the power to bring rain, in season, because of its direct association with the Buddha.

above This Kandyan dancer wears elaborate traditional costume for the Esala Perahera, the 10-day Procession of the Tooth festival, thought to have originated in the third century BC as a rain-seeking ceremony.

right top Elephant tusks guard the silvered doors to the temple wherein the tooth relic is kept. The relic is now kept within a golden casket and never leaves the temple.

right The lake beside the temple was constructed in 1807 by flooding rice fields and is edged with the Walakulu cloud wall. During festivals, the spaces within the walls are illuminated by lamps which send light dancing across the water, to spectacular effect.

Hiroshima Peace Memorial Park

Hiroshima, Japan

Hiroshima is the largest city in the Chugoku region of Honshu, the largest of Japan's islands. The region has a mild climate, but an angry volcanic belly means that earthquakes are not unusual. During the Second World War, on August 6, 1945, the city faced an event that would change its history for ever. The United States Air Force bomber, Enola Gay, flew overhead and dropped the world's first atomic bomb on an unsuspecting population of almost 300,000. The force of the blast was of unnatural ferocity and suddenness. Many were killed instantly, birds exploded in mid-flight; the flash tattooed patterns of clothing on to skin, shapes of bodies on to brickwork and a shadow of shame fell across the history of mankind. Survivors are called hibakushas – 'explosion-affected people'. In 2008 there were 243,692 fitting this description, each with that nightmare etched upon their souls.

Nevertheless, glimmers of hope are being fanned to life by the passage of time. In the Hiroshima Peace Memorial Park, brightly coloured paper cranes have found their way into the language of

peace. Crisply folded in Japanese origami tradition, they trace back to a girl called Sadako Sasaki. The two-year-old showed no initial signs of injury after the A-bomb monstrosity, but nine years later she developed leukaemia. She set about making paper cranes, in the belief that they would cure her. Her death was the catalyst for a monument to peace and prayers for the restful repose of all children killed by the bomb. This pacific message has flown across the earth and returns in the 10 million cranes that are sent annually from hopeful people the world over. On August 6 each year, Japan holds the Hiroshima Peace Memorial Ceremony, a day when people come to the Memorial Cenotaph to honour the dead, comfort the hibakushas and pray for world peace. The ceremony includes ritual acts of dedication, respect and contemplation, with the tolling of a bell and the release of doves – the universal sign of peace. Each year the Mayor of Hiroshima makes a peace declaration. During the 2008 ceremony, Mayor Tadatoshi Akiba announced a two-year study into the emotional effects of the bomb blast, stating that 'it should

above left and right At the Hiroshima Peace Memorial Ceremony, incense is burned and thousands of coloured lanterns are floated on the Motoyasu River in memory of those who died or were damaged by the atomic bomb on August 6, 1945. Many threw themselves into the river at the time of the blast.

teach the important truth, born of tragedy and suffering, that the only role for nuclear weapons is to be abolished.'

With this abolition in mind, Mayors for Peace is an international movement calling for, among other things, a concrete road map to a nuclear-weapon-free world: 2,368 city members worldwide have signed up to this Hiroshima-Nagasaki Protocol. It aims for a significant reversal of that horror, turning the event's impact upon itself to send a positive reaction back to the world. If we can arrive at this end point by 2020, as hoped, we will have begun to move forward.

above Buddhist monks join the prayers held by the Atom Bomb Dome. The Peace Memorial Ceremony begins at 8 am; 15 minutes later the Peace Bell is rung as sirens throughout the city shout a stark reminder of the moment when the bomb struck. This is followed by one minute's silence across the country.

top right A woman stands in quiet prayer before the Memorial Cenotaph. This landmark symbolically shelters the souls of the victims, whose names are recorded here, along with the legend 'Repose ye in Peace, for the error shall not be repeated'.

above This photograph shows the skeletal form of the Atom Bomb Dome, one of the few buildings to have been left standing in the aftermath of the Hiroshima bomb.

Holy Week
Seville, Spain

The Sacred Journey of Seville takes place during Holy Week, known in Spain as Semana Santa, in an event where crush and hush mingle with the sweet smell of orange blossom that hangs thick in the air. The event consists of up to 60 processions that collectively mark and reconstruct Christ's journey through the days leading up to His death and resurrection, from Palm Sunday to Easter Day, and the events that occurred during that time. Hundreds of thousands of people crowd the city streets to witness and take part in this astonishing mixture of devotion, contemplation and, finally, celebration. For the pilgrims and participants, there are many facets to this journey of emotional extremes.

Cofradías and *hermandades* (lay brotherhoods) are the religious brethren who run the event; some of these fraternities date back to the thirteenth century. Participants, more than 2,000 men and women in some processions, walk wearing the cloak, hood and mask of penitents, in the Spanish tongue *penitentes* or *nazarenos*. The penitents act out a public display of contrition, rueing their sins and asking forgiveness in this most holy of Christian seasons. They carry or accompany the *pasos*, huge floats that bear *imagenes*, or religious imagery. These images may be carvings of allegorical scenes based on biblical accounts of Holy Week, of Christ or of the Virgin Mary, according to the theme of the procession. For example, La Borriquita (The Donkey) marks Christ's entry into Jerusalem on a donkey on Palm Sunday, and the *imagenes* narrate that tale among swaying palm branches.

While each differently-named procession is a dramatic event, it is also a deeply spiritual act. Carrying these weighty structures shows solidarity with Christ's suffering during Holy Week, and those who carry crosses do so to feel something of His burden and anguish along the struggle that led to crucifixion. The atmosphere varies from procession to procession. Some walk barefoot, perhaps in silence, and the onlookers follow their example; others are accompanied by singing or cacophonous music. And the distance the processions travel varies too, for the point of departure is the parish church. This means that some people walk for up to 14 hours, through daylight and into the night. El Silencio is a procession that moves in total silence, through streets dimmed by nightfall and the shutting off of street lamps and shop lights. The enclosing darkness and

left Holy Week in Seville sees up to 2,000 *penitentes* acting out a breathtaking public display of contrition as they walk through the streets dressed in hoods and masks. Many walk barefoot and carry *cirios*, the very long candles we can see here. The whole event is dense with symbolism and tradition, the air thick with incense and the scent of orange blossom.

palpable quiet brings an eeriness to the normally bustling streets. This change in mood triggers a sharpened perception of what is happening and of its link to the historical event being honoured. Time is compressed and transformed so that the crowd in Seville becomes the crowd in Jerusalem, watching Jesus' journey all those years ago. Candle flames cast a poignant light as incense rises with prayer. The week ends with just one procession on Easter Day, El Resucitado, the joyful celebration of Christ's resurrection from the dead, His triumph over darkness and evil. The faithful may now return to the world cleansed of their sins and secure in God's love.

below Thousands of people flock to see the *paso* (float) arrive for the Vigil of La Macarena. More formally known as Nuestra Señora de la Esperanza, the Virgin of Hope, the sixteenth-century wooden statue kept in the Basilica depicts a tearful figure grieving the death of her son on Good Friday, the day of the overnight vigil and procession.

below La Soledad de San Lorenzo takes place on Easter Eve. The watching crowd falls silent when the *paso* passes by. Some processions are walking in complete silence; the participants speak to no one when wearing their vestments. The pointed hoods are called *capirote* and represent repentance for sins. The procession is led by *monaguillos*, children dressed as priests who hand out sweets.

The Golden Temple

Amritsar, Punjab, India

What could look more celebratory or elaborately alluring than this splendour of gleaming marble and gilding, all silkily reflected in the Pool of Nectar? Cover your head, remove your shoes and wash your feet. Now you may enter the Harmandir Sahib, named thus in 2005 but still fondly known by many as the Golden Temple. It is said to occupy the place at which Valmiki wrote the epic *Ramayana*, and where he buried the pot of healing amrit from which these sacred waters flowed. Mendicant monks and sages came here for meditation and discourse, and it said that the Buddha too favoured its felicity and spent some years here.

Two thousand years later the philosopher and sage Guru Nanak followed in that great tradition. Then, due to the site's illustrious visitors and inherent auspiciousness, it grew in sanctity and became the foremost destination among the now growing Sikh community. Construction of the temple began in 1574 and was completed in 1601. Its present appearance, however, is the result of evolution as it has been embellished and repaired over the years. Pilgrims and tourists rub shoulders here without distinction or hierarchy. All are welcome and are swept up in the sacred atmosphere and generous embrace. Monumental sculptures, exquisite artworks and patterned floors combine to form a mesmerizing visual feast, leading the eye into the realm of spiritual journey. The faithful bend to touch the floor with their foreheads, humbling themselves while honouring the sanctity of the site. At the heart of the temple complex is the Golden Temple itself, reached by crossing the Guru's Bridge, a journey symbolic of the soul's passage when leaving this world after death. The 62-metre (203-foot) marble causeway funnels crowds into the Pardakshna, or circular path, that allows for sunwise circling of the temple, the doors of which open onto four directions, reconfirming that it welcomes comers from any quarter.

Shimmering with copper, gold and precious jewels, the luxury of the building heralds the treasure kept within – the sacred text, Guru Granth Sahib, which is recited all day in the continuous ceremony called Akhand Path. Each night the Guru Granth Sahib is ritually carried back across the waters via the silver doors of the Guru Bridge, to its 'bed' in the Akal Takht. This journey is fuelled by sacred song, prayer and all the sounds and scents of fervent worship, and is broadcast throughout the country. The temple is host to any number of celebrations and festivals that mark rites of passage for the individual, seasons and occasions relevant to the faith. Most Sikhs come here at least once during their lifetime, wherever they live, with many making the journey to mark significant occasions in their lives. Up to two million people may visit at Deepavali (Diwali), when flames and fireworks celebrate and symbolize the light which inhabits every heart.

previous page A Sikh pilgrim sits by the calm waters of the Pool of Nectar, contemplating the silky reflections of the majestic Golden Temple. Across the water, hundreds line up to cross to the pilgrim destination, which they will circle before entering. This tradition was first established in 1574, although the sacred pool has been a focal point for ascetics, priests and philosophers from very early times.

left above Thirsty pilgrims receive sweet water outside the temple complex. Amritsar is known for its hospitality. All are welcome to visit the temple regardless of their colour, creed or status. This is symbolized by the building complex having doors open to every direction, welcoming the north, south, east and west.

left below Pilgrims on the Guru's Bridge are eager to reach the Golden Temple, the point of arrival. Within the temple they will hear words from the sacred texts before departing and returning to the world, transformed by the experience of being among these hallowed spaces, and having taken part in the sacred ceremonies.

right A volunteer serves refreshments to visitors. All who come here are invited to share in a meal offered freely by the temple authorities, prepared and delivered by volunteers who seek to serve others. Sikhs strive to balance worship and charity in their lives and the temple, or gurdwara, is the hub of their community.

The Jani Festival
Latvia

The Jani Festival is an exuberant midsummer celebration which has come to represent Latvian identity and marks the sun's sacred journey across the sky. Within many cultures, fire is a symbol of purification and renewal. It can also be the destroyer that allows new life; it is seen as apotropaic – the domestic fire of the ancient hearths was never allowed to die as it could drive away evil. And above all, fire represents the sun, which in turn is the symbol of God.

Christianity arrived in Latvia from Germany during the twelfth century and was met with resistance; the ancient religion here was agricultural, and it is still deeply embedded in Latvian culture. Agricultural cycles are dominated by the heavenly bodies; the rhythm of life is thus mapped and ordered by the rise and fall of the sun, its daily journey across the sky, its solstices and equinoxes. Jani is the festival that marks the summer solstice, when the sun reaches its zenith, and Janis is the ancient Latvian god of this occasion.

Although the festival is of pre-Christian origin, many scholars agree that it takes its name, at least in part, from Saint John's Eve, the eve of celebration before the feast day of Saint John the Baptist, and so is a blending of the old faith with the new. John the Baptist is often associated in Christianity with diminishing daylight, which begins at summer solstice. This is because, as Christ's forerunner, he yielded and waned as Christ eclipsed him and grew in strength. Therefore, Christ's birth is marked during the dark months, when light begins its annual regrowth. For the Latvian people the festival is a time for celebration expressed through feasting, drinking and singing. Men take the name Janis (John) for the occasion and wear wreaths of oak leaves on their heads. The oak tree is a symbol of power and masculinity. Furthermore, its ability to attract lightning is a form of contagious magic; coming from the sun, lightning consecrates the oak tree with its sacred strength. Thus in crowning themselves with oak leaves, the men assume those attributes. The women's garlands include linden blossom. This is the counterbalance to the oak; it is feminine, associated with water and possessing of healing powers. Dainas are traditional Latvian folksongs reserved for the festival and they tell of the cosmic bonds between nature, the human world and the realm of the supernatural. While these are sung, folk dances are stepped and circled. Special foods, such as cheese made with carawya seeds and known as jana siars, are eaten and jani beer enjoyed. But fire is the focus of the event. Huge bonfires crackle and spark, spit and smoulder, casting the age-old spell of fascination that has captured human imaginings since the dawn of time. Around its flames stories are told and laughter is shared as people draw close to celebrate its presence and feel its warmth, while enjoying the shortest night. This marks the triumph of day over night and light over darkness. As the sun begins to rise and the fire sinks down, young men leap across the flames to confirm their manhood and the women wash their faces in the potent morning dew.

right The Jani Festival marks the summer solstice, with celebrations continuing throughout midsummer night. Feasting, storytelling, singing and dancing pass the hours, marking the triumph of light over dark. The tradition dates from the ancient Latvian calendar which turned around agricultural seasons, and was therefore dominated by the solar cycles.

above Seeds are thrown into the fire by girls wearing traditional crowns of flowers, including linden blossom for its feminine and healing qualities. The men wear the oak leaves of heroes around their heads, for the oak's strength and durability. They leap through the fire to confirm their masculinity.

above Fire is central to Jani celebrations. It symbolizes purification, renewal and cleansing, and represents the sun. It also drives away evil and danger. Together these positive forces symbolize God's presence on earth.

The Konark Sun Temple
Orissa, India

The small town of Konark resides in the Puri district of Orissa on the Bay of Bengal. It used to be situated on the coast, but the sea has drawn back over time and so Konark is now 2 kilometres (1¼ miles) inland. The area is buffeted by monsoons, cyclones and tidal waves. Over time, sands and jungle hid this great structure, but conservation work began in the twentieth century and the temple is now accessible and in a more stable condition than it once was.

This is where King Narasimhadeva I (1236–64) had black granite fashioned into an immense temple in honour of the sun god Surya. It is made to resemble the 24-wheeled chariot in which the sun races across the sky drawn by seven horses. The seven horses represent the days of the week, twelve pairs of wheels are for the months of the year and the eight spokes within the wheels are the divisions within a woman's day. Thus the chariot stands in honour of the sun god's power over time. Its position points east towards the rising sun over the Bay of Bengal, and the horses would pull the sun over the sea at daybreak to launch it on its skyward journey.

The surface of the temple is carved with exquisite detail. Intricate lace-like fashioning belies the might of the stone but eloquently describes deities, flora and fauna, scenes from the Kama Sutra, beasts from mythology and beasts of the sea. It is said that the tower used to contain powerful lodestones which were employed to make the King's throne levitate in the air, and that the strength of the magnets caused ships to lose their way by interrupting tidal patterns and befuddling the ships' compasses. The Portuguese took the magnets away and now they languish in the realm of legend.

In February each year, pilgrim visitors come, many on foot, to celebrate the Magha Saptami (Sun Festival), which is also known as Chandrabhaga Mela. This is the temple's most-visited festival and a time for worshipping the sun god. The event celebrates the solar rebirth, as it stretches the hours of daylight and extends its path above the horizon on its return to Uttarayana, its northern course. The congregation bathes in the sacred river Chandrabhaga, or in the sea, while awaiting the sunrise over the ocean's southeast horizon. And when that great ball of fire lifts itself clear of the water, the zealous splashing of the pilgrims throws into the air a million sparkling drops that collide with shouts of praise and joyful laughter. This is followed by a walk to the temple, where the worshippers circle the chariot clockwise to follow the path of the sun itself. Once the rituals

right This is one of the wheels on the Sun Temple at Konark, which is designed to resemble a huge chariot for the sun god to travel in as he crosses the dawn sky. It is positioned to face the rising sun over the Bay of Bengal.

are completed, the rest of the day is spent feasting in the joyful company of friends until the sun dips back below the horizon and darkness enfolds the temple. The sun god has fulfilled his promise and all is well. Tomorrow he will bless the land with warmth and light again.

left Sunlight strikes the Sun Temple. Intricate, filigree carvings grace the walls. Friezes show scenes from the Kama Sutra, tales from mythology and creatures from land and sea. At one time, mariners around this coastline used the temple's tower for navigation, but ceased when shipwrecks were blamed on the temple's supposed powers to affect the tides.

above This view through the temple chariot, built during the thirteenth century, shows the splendour of the design and construction. Famed for being the best in the region, the delicate tracery, pleasing proportions, curvilinear towers and cupolas all add up to a mesmerizing glory which fills the pilgrim with spellbound awe, touching the spirit through the eye.

Stonehenge
Wiltshire, England

We may never know why Salisbury Plain was chosen as the site for Stonehenge, just as we may never know the monument's original name or fully grasp its function. But our understanding of the circle changes over time as scholars and archaeologists make new findings. The henge was built in three stages – the name 'henge' coming from the verb 'to hang'. First, using tools of bone and antler, a ditch and bank were made and timbers set within, dating to 3,100 BC. Then around 2,500 BC huge bluestones were fetched from Wales. The monoliths were dragged and floated for more than 400 kilometres (248 miles), an almost magical feat of might and management. Two hundred years after that the five-ton bluestones were rearranged into a horseshoe and encircled by a ring of massive sarsen stones. These were hewn with joints to lock the lintels, bracing pairs into trilithons, the stones lifted by some miracle we cannot fathom.

left Alignments within the stone circle of Stonehenge mark positions and movements of the heavenly bodies, making temporal points tangible and their arrival calculable. But still there is speculation as to why exactly people came here. Druidic ceremony marks the summer solstice now.

below The midsummer dawn is greeted at Stonehenge by an eager crowd for whom this is a special and spectacular occasion.

How the stones were used is hard to pinpoint too. Burials near the site are of travellers, from the Alps and beyond, and animals were brought from far away – were they trade, gifts or sustenance? The gatherings were extensive and it is thought that sites nearby were used as pilgrim accommodation. But still there is speculation as to why exactly people came here. Alignments within the circle are clear markers of heavenly bodies and it is most likely that summer and winter solstices were celebrated here. Midsummer and midwinter are located on this calendar, temporal points made tangible, and their arrival calculable. And it may be that lunar eclipses were predicted, using long-lost knowledge. Season and time's reassuring patterns are well worth celebration and always

have been; after all, they bring our sustenance. The all-seeing sky, casting light and rain, has always been looked to for omens, its planetary messages decoded. And perhaps this is why the stones were arranged in a complete circle. Walking within a ring of stones is to immerse oneself in a calibration machine, reading stone against sky against star. Heaven is brought within an earthly framework, earthly forms pressed against a celestial backdrop. Sink to your knees and the stones rise higher. What a delight!

And what mysteries were discovered and debated here? As we have seen elsewhere, a circle is a sign of harmony, infinity and perfection. It can also be used to ward off evil, hence bracelets and belts act as personal talismans. In cultures where illness is

seen as the work of malice, the circle takes on a curative role. A disproportionate number of the dead buried around Stonehenge show signs of illness and injury, and many fragments of bluestone have been found chipped away as if to be taken as amulets – portable doses of remedial stone. So perhaps Stonehenge was a place of healing, alongside its cosmic role. Today access to the stones is strictly limited, due to the number of visitors who come here, and the passions roused by those who would use its power and those who would protect it. However, out of hours access can be applied for, under special circumstances. Still a place of wonder, it is the ultimate destination for British neo-druids whose predecessors have greeted the summer solstice here for up to 800 years.

above left This is not the world's largest stone circle, but it is the only one with lintels along the top, and in this it is unique. The lintels were hoisted, by some unknown method, to brace the pairs into trilithons. It is thought that the name 'henge' comes from the Anglo Saxon verb 'to hang', thus a reference to the horizontal stones suspended by the verticals.

above This character, who is called Arthur, king of the druids, leads a torchlit procession on Midsummer's Night. These celebrations date to long ago, when it was thought that plants had extra healing powers; they were picked overnight by herbalists in preparation for what might lie ahead. Bonfires drove away evil which might stalk the land, now that the sun was shortening its path along the horizon.

Lindisfarne
England

Lindisfarne is a place of raw, intense beauty, where vibrant light bounces off the North Sea and foamy waves thunder against pale sand. Home to myriad sea birds, sleek and comical, rare and commonplace, here crisp wind fills the vibrant air and sets the pulse racing. This tidal island in the northeast of England is also known as Holy Island. It serves as a retreat for those who seek respite and wish to withdraw into a period of isolation for spiritual healing or deeper understanding.

It was Saint Aiden who, around AD 635, came here from the isle of Iona to establish a monastery at King Oswald's request. Later on, Saint Cuthbert became prior and enlarged the community. His reputation for wisdom and healing grew as he took missionary journeys across the north of England. Although he left his mark on many places, it is Lindisfarne that is most closely associated with his ministry, and it is Lindisfarne that lends its name to the book of Gospels that is famed throughout Christendom. This exquisite work, produced during the early eighth century, is one of the island's gifts to the world. The artist-calligrapher was probably a monk called Eadfrith, who wove Anglo Saxon tradition with Celtic understanding to make this unique and precious object, in honour of Saint Cuthbert. During AD 793 the *Anglo-Saxon Chronicle* recorded omens warning of terrible things to come: whirlwinds, lightning and dragons preceded famine, and then Lindisfarne was raided by Vikings. It was a cruel and bloody attack. The monks fled inland, taking with them what they could, including the late Cuthbert's body.

Today the monastery stands in ruin but the spiritual presence of Aiden, Cuthbert and their brethren is still tangible; in fact, their presence is felt more keenly than their absence. This spiritual quality is maintained by those who have stepped into the footprints of the monks. The parish church of Saint Mary the Virgin ministers to residents and pilgrims alike, and there is evidence that it occupies the site of Aiden's first, wooden monastery. The island heaves with groups of walkers during the summer months; spiritual tourists, hikers, seekers of wildlife and artists wait for low tide and step across the ancient pilgrim route. Their visits are timed to ebb and flow with the sea for the sake of safe passage. And each year during Holy Week, five pilgrim routes converge on Holy Island: this is the ecumenical pilgrimage of the Northern Cross. Walkers carry large crosses over distances of 112 to 193 kilometres (70 to 120 miles), coming together to reach the island on the morning of Good Friday. On Easter Eve, driftwood is collected from the beaches for the Paschal Fire, symbolizing Christ's presence as light in the world. On Easter morning the pilgrims' crosses are taken, decked with flowers, into the church for a celebratory service, after which the congregation makes a joyful procession around the village. This act of witness is a proclamation of faith and a link with pilgrims past. After the hard walk that brought them here, they return to the world walking on air, lifted by the joys of Easter.

left Lindisfarne Priory on Holy Island serves as a spiritual retreat for those seeking to deepen their faith and touch the sanctity generated by Cuthbert and those who followed him. The rhythms of the tide set the pace of life here, throwing the pilgrim directly into nature's hands in an ancient synchrony.

right Walking barefoot across the wet sands, pilgrims approach Holy Island as the tide holds back. The tall posts mark the safe route, symbolic of spiritual guidance. Writers in the twenty-first century continue the island's tradition of spiritual literature, first made famous with the Lindisfarne Gospels. Today's books on Celtic Christianity guide pilgrims when they return to the mainland.

Sultan Ahmed Mosque
Istanbul, Turkey

Known also as the Blue Mosque for the blue Iznik tiles inside, this building is famed for its six minarets. It was made for Sultan Ahmet, reputedly to rival the Byzantine Hagia Sophia that stands nearby, and it is thought to be the last great work of Ottoman classical architecture. Begun in 1609, it took seven years to build; sadly, Sultan Ahmet died a year later, aged only 27. He rests outside with his wife and three sons.

The exterior of the structure is majestic and triumphant. The minarets soar heavenwards, their spear-like forms in sharp contrast to the billowing cupolas that cluster around the central dome. Upon entry, modestly dressed visitors cover their heads and remove their shoes. The most delightful way to enter is through the west door and this is reserved for worshippers; tourists must enter from the north and stoop beneath the hanging chains as an act of humility. Once inside, the architecture imposes itself upon the senses. A sublime abundance of mesmeric pattern runs across tiles, windows, arches and prayer mats. Curves echo arches, rings of windows encircle great hoops of lamps, and organic forms lace themselves around fluted pillars and stained-glass windows.

The splendour of this is expressive of Allah's infinite goodness; the power of the domes sends energy inwards to touch the worshipper's inner core. Worship is, of course, one of the central duties, or 'five pillars' of Islam. And the daily cycle designates five times for prayer, which are announced by the mu'adhdhin from a minaret. Prayer may be solitary or communal, with all men being required to attend the midday prayers on Fridays. Surrounding this is a larger calendar of festivals and commemoration, including Ramadan. This period of fasting covers the ninth month of the Islamic year. Many of the faithful stay in the mosque for the last 10 days of Ramadan, to be there for the Laylat al-Qadr, or Night of Power, when angels and the Spirit come down; it is the most auspicious time to focus on prayer, learning and duty. The night is also associated with the delivery to the Prophet Mohammad of the Last Book of Allah. These events must be celebrated and Allah thanked for the strength he sent during fasting.

Fasting ends in feasting and so after Ramadan comes Eid ul-Fitr. This festival begins when the sliver of the new moon's crescent slips into the sky. People dress in their best clothes and come to the mosque, many in procession; the faithful spill from the mosque and pray outside. This is also a time for forgiveness, gift-giving, family reunions and acts of charity. Bridges of friendship are built or mended, family bonds strengthened. Those who were in retreat must now re-adjust to the bustle of everyday life. Returning to the world, its patterns of eating, working and interacting with others, is to emerge from the spiritual realm to the earthly one. From discipline comes freedom and the necessary balance between the two.

left The interior of the mosque is sumptuously elegant. Natural daylight and circles of lamps echo the domes and arches in a play of curves and columns. Within these walls, prayer rises and is magnified by sacred architecture and patterning, all designed to the glory of God. Roughly 20,000 blue Iznik tiles give the mosque its popular name, the Blue Mosque.

previous pages The Sultan Ahmed Mosque's six minarets caused consternation when the building was finished, as it was seen to rival the mosque in Mecca. So the latter building was given a seventh minaret to restore its superior status.

above Five times each day, the faithful must turn to Mecca and pray. Until recently, prayer times were announced from a minaret by the muezzin, who would make his way up to the top via a spiral staircase. Now, however, the call rings across the city from loudspeakers. At dusk, coloured floodlights play across the outside of the building.

The Taizé Community
Saône-et-Loire, France

It was Brother Roger who founded this ecumenical monastic community with the objective of reconciliation both in the Christian church, and throughout the world. It takes its name from the village in southern France in which it is situated. Young people in particular are encouraged in prayer, bible study and communal work, with more than 100,000 making pilgrimages here each year.

Coming from his native Switzerland with the intention of helping war-torn families, the house Brother Roger bought in 1940 soon became a place of sanctuary for many Jewish refugees. However, that changed when the Gestapo occupied the house during 1942, while Roger was away collecting funds. After France was liberated in 1944, he returned to Taizé and his work in the community resumed. Three years later, he and six brethren took vows of celibacy, respect for authority and common property.

As the community grew in numbers, so its message extended throughout the world. The success of its charitable work in places as diverse as Asia, Africa, the Americas and Europe caught the attention of many in those regions. In 1966 the community held its first international meeting for young people and the results of that were built upon, with the doors being opened to any, regardless of their tradition. Today's 100 resident brethren come from 25 different countries. This combination of backgrounds is recognized through a wide range of worship. Music, chanting, silence and singing come in a spectrum of styles and forms, but at the core is the search for Christ in everyday life and a continued yearning for a reconciled church; what unites Christians is considered more important than their differences. Living conditions for pilgrims are simple and visitors are asked to bring a few practical things with them, including a tent if possible. But more importantly, a Bible should be taken, and musicians are invited to bring their instruments in order to share their talents in worship.

While coming to Taizé is a sacred journey in itself, the emphasis is on what the pilgrims take away with them on their return home. Thus a scheme called 'a pilgrimage of trust on Earth' has been established. The idea behind this project is for pilgrims to radiate God's peace in their work and daily lives, meaning that the time spent in Taizé itself should be sewn as seeds of faith in the world beyond the community. A typical day in Taizé is split between prayer, workshops and discussion, with themes chosen according to the age of the participants. Once a year there is a gathering in a major European city, bringing together thousands of young people from across the globe. Between Christmas and New Year they spend their time sharing discussions and airing doubts and values in an atmosphere of trust and peace. Inevitably, though, groups of young people generate excitement and so celebration is never far away, bubbling to the surface in the joy of new friendships, new learning and renewed faith in Christ.

left and below Prayers within the Church of the Reconciliation at Taizé are aided by the soft flicker of candlelight, symbolizing the presence of Christ, the Light of the World. Christians from many backgrounds come here and this ecumenism is reflected in the varied styles of worship. Taizé chants are known throughout the world for their ability to still the mind and so assist prayer.

Santiago De Compostela
Galicia, Spain

Many pilgrim routes lead to Santiago, 11 are well established and all are well used. Some merge with others, some forge ahead alone. The paths cross mountains and plateaux, cities and farms. And the way is marked with milestones, daubed arrows or studs in the pavement. Pilgrims are old and young, walkers and cyclists, zealous Christians and seekers of faith, and the weather does what it pleases, as it always has.

The Way of Saint James, as it is also known, was established during the ninth century, when the relics of the saint were found in a tomb in a field beneath a star. The pilgrimage became popular during the Middle Ages due to the significance of the relics. A chapel was built to mark the site and now the resplendent Cathedral of Santiago de Compostela stands in its place, drawing at least 100,000 people from around the world every year. During Holy Years, when Saint James' feast day falls on a Sunday, the numbers exceed that. Pilgrims carry a 'passport' called the *credencial*, which gets stamped at key stations along the way. This is not only a record of the journey, but entitles pilgrims to stay in the *refugios*, pilgrim-only hostels. It also qualifies holders for an official certificate, a *compostela*, in recognition of their journey.

At journey's end, exhaustion may be allieviated by the sense of achievement that comes with completion. Tired muscles and blistered feet may be soothed and rested. Arrival at the cathedral is a chance to praise God with fellow travellers, give thanks for the blessings received and ask for His help for the future. All of these aspects are present in the pilgrims' rituals and services. The great entrance, the Pórtico da Gloria, is a twelfth-century masterpiece of Romanesque sculpture. The middle column of this is a representation of Saint James, and it is customary for pilgrims to touch his left foot to mark the end of their journey. Here is a place to stop and consider the multitude that, one by one, have laid their hands on this same stone. Next, a walk down the central aisle leads to the saint's relics, which are honoured in prayerful silence, and then around to the statue of the apostle, which may be embraced. Those who wish to make a confession will find a priest to hear them in their own tongue or a common second language. A Pilgrims' Mass is held at noon each day in the cathedral, and those who earned their *compostela* the day before have their starting point and country of origin read out during the service. On feast days the great vessel full of incense, the Botafumeiro, swings from on high, throwing incense in a celebratory arc above the heads of the congregation. On turning to leave, pilgrims may regret the end of the shared camaraderie and parting from newfound friends. But there is the optimism that always follows an accomplishment to hold on to, and the need to discover and live out what has been learned from the journey, from others and from the blessings of Santiago. In that respect, the sacred journey continues.

above Within the cathedral the Botafumeiro swings above the heads of the congregation, sweeping an arc of incense as it scribes an almost semicircular line. The Botafumeiro is suspended from a 400-year-old mechanism in the roof, and at 1.6 metres (5 feet) high, this is one of the largest incense burners in the world, and takes a considerable amount of stoking and controlling.

right The Feast of Saint James is celebrated by thousands of pilgrims who flock to the Plaza del Obradoiro, outside the cathedral. They will have come from all across the Christian world, on foot, horseback, bicycle or a combination of these. This is the most popular festival for the cathedral but by no means the only busy time.

right The approaches to Santiago are varied and pass through many types of landscape. The going is tough and rugged in places, gentle and pretty elsewhere.

right below The eleventh-century bridge, Punta la Reina, was built especially for pilgrims by Queen Urraca of Navarra, helping them on their way across the water to Santiago de Compostela.

far right The high altar is an eruption of jubilant decoration with putti, chandeliers and moulding worked in jasper, silver and other precious materials. Behind the altar, stairs lead up to the thirteenth-century figure of Saint James, allowing pilgrims to climb and kiss his cloak. Thus their pilgrimage here is fulfilled. This end point is the start of a new beginning. Ritual has been observed, prayers uttered and lives changed: it is time to go back to the world.

Index

Figures in italics indicate captions.

Suggested Reading

Alone of All Her Sex: The Myth and the Cult of the Virgin Mary,
Marina Warner, Vintage Books, 1998.

The Atlas of Religion: Mapping Contemporary Challenges and Beliefs,
Joanne O'Brien and Martin Palmer, Earthscan, 2007.

Bright Earth: The Invention of Colour, Philip Ball, Vintage Books, 2008.

Colour: Travels Through the Paintbox, Victoria Finlay, Sceptre, 2003.

The Continuum Encyclopedia of Symbols, Udo Becker, editor,
Continuum International, 2000.

Faith in Conservation: New Approaches to Religions and the Environment,
Martin Palmer with Victoria Finlay, World Bank Publications, 2003.

Gods in the Sky: Astronomy from the Ancients to the Enlightenment,
Allan Chapman, Channel 4 Books, 2002.

Heart for the World, Marcus Braybrooke, O Books, 2006.

The Illustrated Guide to World Religions, Michael D Coogan, editor,
Oxford University Press, 2003.

Islamic Art and Architecture, Robert Hillenbrand, Thames & Hudson, 1999.

Mapping Time: The Calendar and Its History, E.G. Richards, Oxford
University Press, 19989.

*Medieval Views of the Cosmos: Picturing the Universe in the Christian and
Islamic Middle Ages,* Evelyn Edson and Emilie Savage-Smith,
The Bodleian Library, 2004.

The Oxford Companion to World Mythology, David Leeming, Oxford
University Press, 2005.

The Oxford Dictionary of World Religions, John Bowker, editor, Oxford
University Press, 1999.

Pilgrims and Pilgrimage in the Medieval West, Diana Webb,
I B Tauris & Co., 2001.

Places of Power: Measuring the Secret Energy of Ancient Sites,
Paul Deveraux, Cassell, 1999.

Ramayana: A Tale of Gods and Demons, Ranchor Prime, Mandala
Publishing Group, 2008.

Reading Buddhist Art: An Illustrated Guide to Buddhist Signs and Symbols,
Meher McArthur, Thames & Hudson, 2002.

Sacred: People of the Book – Judaism, Christianity, Islam, John Reeve,
editor, British Library, 2007.

*Sacred Britain: A Guide to the Sacred Pilgrim Routes of England, Scotland
and Wales,* Martin Palmer and Nigel Palmer, Piatkus Books, 1997.

Sacred Earth, Sacred Stones: Spiritual Sites and Landscapes, Brian Leigh
Molyneaux and Piers Vitebsky, Duncan Baird, 2001.

The Sacred East, C. Scott Littleton, editor, Duncan Baird, 1999.

Sacred Imagery, Judith Millidge, World Publications, 1999.

Wanderlust: A History of Walking, Rebecca Solnit, Verso Books, 2006.

The World of Pilgrimage, G W Target, Automobile Association, 1997.

World Religions: A Comprehensive Guide to Religions of the World,
Martin Palmer, Times Books, 2002.

Picture Credits

The publishers would like to thank the following sources
for their kind permission to reproduce the pictures in this book.
Key: t=Top, b=Bottom, c=Centre, l=Left and r=Right

Front Endpapers: Getty Images/AFP/Toru Yamanaka
Back Endpapers: Corbis/Christophe Boisvieux

4Corners Images: /Morandi Bruno: 141t; /Johanna Huber: 207r, 244; /Borchi Massimo: 136, 207l, 232-233; /Schmid Reinhard: 130-131; /Giovanni Simeone: 242-243, 245 **Alamy**: /©A.P: 228-229, 230; /©AfriPics.com: 48-49; /©Rex Allen: 137l; /©Nir Alon: 45l; /©Stephen Bardens: 176; /©Tibor Bognar: 84t; /©Kevin Galvin: 132; /©Eddie Gerald: 145t; /©Terry Harris/Just Greece Photo Library: 104; /©Geoff A Howard: 85; /©Imagestate Media Partners Limited – Impact Photos: 24-25, 171b; /©Indiapicture: 74; /©isifa Image Service s.r.o: 50, 88-89; /©Israel images: 53, 55; /©JTB Photo Communications: 60r, 84b; /©Ben King: 96; /©Melvyn Longhurst: 66; /©Look Die Bildagentur der Fotografen GmbH: 12l, 21, 22b, 168-169, 171t; /©David Lyons: 22t; /©Neil McAllister: 75, 170-171; /©Bruce Miller: 2-3; /©Paul O'Connor: 28, 29; /©Graeme Peacock: 241; /©Mark Pearson: 183; /©Photolibrary Wales: 110r, 148-149; /©PhotoStock-Israel: 5, 45r; /©Profimedia International s.r.o: 100, 134; /©Reuters: 133t; /©Stephen Saks Photography: 97; /©David Sanger Photography: 111r, 142-143; /©Jack Sullivan: 51; /©Jim Zuckerman: 234 **Alinari Archives** – Florence: 32 **Apollo Images**: 40 **Art Directors and TRIP:** 77, 175t, 182; /Ark Religion: 43t **Br Lawrence Lew, O.P.**: 128 **Brenda Tharp**: 198 **Bronek Kaminski**: 116, 212, 213, 214r **Chris Strickland**: 16r **Corbis**: 61l, 86-87; /©Jon Arnold: 135; /©Sharna Balfour: 47; /©Anthony Bannister: 13r, 46; /©Dave Bartruff: 4; /©Yannis Behrakis/Reuters: 106; /©Amit Bhargava: 164t; /©Christophe Boisvieux: 162, 166, 167, 206l, 215t, 246, 247; /©Massimo Borchi: 69t; /Stephanie Colasanti: 68; /©Richard A. Cooke: 204-205; /©David Cumming: 248; /©Keith Dannemiller: 199; /©Marcelo Del Pozo/Reuters: 222; /©Mark Downey/Lucid Images: 79; /©Robert Estall: 192, 193t&b; /©Michael Freeman: 108-109; /110l, 111l, 118-119, 123, 124; /©Lowell Georgia: 20; /©Gianni Giansanti: 184b; /©Peter Guttman: 156t; /©Ali Haider: 38; /©Jon Hicks: 35, 214l; /©Jim Hollander: 52; /©Jeremy Horner: 7, 127, 211t; /©Rob Howard: 64; /©John R. Jones: 137r; /©David Keaton: 9, 208; /©Manjunath Kiran: 163; /©Richard Klune: 219t; /©Frans Lanting: 160l, 172-173; /©Frederic Larson: 186-187; /©Xurxo S. Lobato: 251; /©Christophe Loviny: 125; /©Christopher J. Morris: 60l, 64t&b; /©Mike Nelson: 41; /©Kazuyoshi Nomachi: 42, 43b; /©Paulo Novias: 185, 184t; /©Richard T. Nowitz: 54-55; /©Caroline Penn: 94-95; /©James Pomerantz: 165t; /©Vittoriano Rastelli: 10-11, 31; /©Reuters: 12r, 39, 93t&b, 157, 179b; /©Michael Reynolds: 141b; /©Galen Rowell: 62; /©Hamid Sardar: 140; /©Phil Schermeister: 190-191; /©Frédéric Soltan/Sygma: 67, 72-73, 235; /©Paul Souders: 175b; /©Roman Soumar: 152-153; /©Penny Tweedie: 15t&b; /©Patrick Ward: 223; /©Nancy G. Western Photography: 190; /©Nik Wheeler: 156b; /©John Henry Claude Wilson/Robert Harding Images: 37, 76; /©Peter M.Wilson: 105; /©Adam Woolfitt: 250b; /©Alison Wright: 194; /©Marilyn Angel Wynn: 161r, 189; /©Michael S. Yamashita: 126l; /©Korczak Ziolkowski: 188; **DanitaDelimont.com**: /©Bill Bachmann: 138-139; /©David Bartruff: 82; /©Kalpana Kartik: 180 **Document Iran:** /Mohammad Kheirkhah: 160r, 179t **Fotolibra:** /Theodorus Antonatos: 154; /Sean W. Burges: 30; / Swen Connrad/YumeVision: 195; /Dino Fracchia: 206r, 220-221; /Geoff France: 129; /

Hanan Isachar: 13l, 18-19; /Karen Kelly: 202r **Getty Images:** 26, 120, 121; /AFP: 23, 44, 69b, 92, 150, 151, 216, 216-217, 226t, 239; /Aurora: 90-91; /DEA/M.Borchi: 98, 99, 101l&r; /Macduff Everton: 200-201; /Martin Gray: 178; /Gavin Gough: 36; /©George Grall/National Geographic: 197; /©Sylvain Grandadam: 61r, 102; /Frans Lemmens: 34; /Peter Macdiarmid: 237; /Bruno Morandi: 158-159, 161l, 180-181; /©Jim Richardson: 56-57; /Uriel Sinai: 145b; /Mario Tama: 164b, 165b; /Yoshio Tomii: 219b; /Travel Ink: 70-71; /Gordon Wiltsie/National Geographic: 210 **Gutner:** 1 **Imagestate:** /Peter Menzel: 81 **In Vision Images:** 107 **Isabella Tree:** 112l&r, 113 **JTB Photo Communications**: 83, 122 **Jean-Marc Giboux:** 78 **Jeremy Sutton-Hibbert:** 218-219 **John Cleare:** 203 **Lonely Planet Images:** /Richard l'Anson: 227; /Sara-Jane Cleland: 27; /Christopher Herwig: 8, 250t; **Ludmila Ketslakh Photography:** 16l **Masterfile:** /©Theo Allofs: 58-59 **Michael Hughes:** 117l&r **Mira Terra Images:** /Paul Skelcher: 209; /Kymri Wilt: 148 **Murray-Darling Basin Commission:** /Arthur Mostead: 14 **National Geographic Stock:** /Gordon Gahan: 17 **Paul Souders:** /WorldFoto: 126r **Photolibrary:** /Charles Bowman: 202l, 215b; /Jeremy Bright: 226b; /Robin Bush: 196; /Mark Cator: 238-239; /DEA/F Galardi: 174; /Robert Gallagher: 144; /Rosine Mazin: 103; /Jean-Baptiste Rabouan: 177; /Don Smith: 211b; /Vidler Vidler: 240; /Adam Woolfitt: 236-237; /Alison Wright: 63 **Photoshot:** /Imagebroker: 155; /UPPA: 133b; /World Pictures: 145-146 **Reuters:** /Ints Kalnins: 231 **Rex Features:** /Sipa Press: 249 **Riccardo De Luca:** 33b **Robert Harding Picture Library:** /©Eitan Simanor: 224-225 **Scala**, Florence: 33t **Steve Davey**: 80 **Three Blind Men Photography**: /Dominic Sansoni: 114, 115

Every effort has been made to acknowledge correctly and contact the source and/or copyright holder of each picture and Carlton Books Limited apologizes for any unintentional errors or omissions which will be corrected in future editions of this book.

Author Acknowledgements

Warm thanks for help and encouragement to:
Sue Booys, Richard Booys, Brian Catling, John Crowe, Lisa Dyer and her team at Carlton, Ann Hind, David Owen, Adam Papaphilippopoulos, Athanasios Papaphilippopoulos, Tila Rodriguez-Past, Sarah Simblet, and most especially, Holly Slingsby and Tom Slingsby.